高等学校旅游专业系列教材

新编旅游英语

主　编　郭　婷　艾治国
副主编　张　松　曹继宏
　　　　王艳滨　李佳玉

哈尔滨工业大学出版社

内 容 提 要

本书是一本内容全面、实用性强的旅游英语教材。全书共10个单元,主要包括:预定机票、海关、娱乐活动、邮政局、酒店服务、家外之家、中国美食、中国茶、观光、旅游购物等方面的内容。

本书可作为高等学校旅游管理及相关专业的教材,也适合于旅游业人员自修、培训及英语专业学生泛读使用。

图书在版编目(CIP)数据

新编旅游英语/郭婷,艾治国主编. —2版. —哈尔滨:哈尔滨工业大学出版社,2008.6(2020.9重印)
(高等学校旅游专业系列教材)
ISBN 978-7-5603-2187-5

Ⅰ.新… Ⅱ.①郭… ②艾… Ⅲ.旅游-英语-高等学校-教材 Ⅳ.H31

中国版本图书馆 CIP 数据核字(2008)第 129254 号

责任编辑　杨　桦　杨明蕾
封面设计　卞秉利
出版发行　哈尔滨工业大学出版社
社　　址　哈尔滨市南岗区复华四道街 10 号　邮编 150006
传　　真　0451-86414749
网　　址　http://hitpress.hit.edu.cn
印　　刷　哈尔滨圣铂印刷有限公司
开　　本　787mm×960mm　1/16　印张 13　字数 235 千字
版　　次　2005 年 9 月第 1 版　2008 年 6 月第 2 版
　　　　　2020 年 9 月第 8 次印刷
书　　号　ISBN 978-7-5603-2187-5
定　　价　28.00 元

(如因印装质量问题影响阅读,我社负责调换)

总　　序

随着我国经济体制改革的不断深入，旅游业一跃成为我国的朝阳产业、支柱产业。旅游业的蓬勃发展，促进了旅游教育的繁荣。截止2002年年底，全国共有旅游类高等院校（包括设有旅游系或旅游专业的院校）407所，比上年增长30.99%，在校生157 409人，增长54%。即使这样，仍然不能满足旅游业发展的需要。

旅游业是综合性很强的产业，同时也是一种文化性产业。尤其是我国入世以来，旅游业对从业人员的素质要求越来越高，已由满足上岗要求转变为适应行业发展的需求，由单纯的岗位技能掌握拓展为综合应用能力的具备。因而，旅游业对高等院校旅游专业的培养目标提出了全新的要求，其教材建设就显得十分重要。

本套教材是遵循系统阐述基础理论、基本知识，并紧密结合生产、经营和管理实际的原则，组织黑龙江大学、哈尔滨商业大学、哈尔滨师范大学、黑龙江工程学院等十几所院校教师编写的。本套教材包括《旅游学概论》、《酒店管理》、《旅游服务教程》等16种书。

本套教材具备四大突出的特点：

第一，结合旅游专业的培养目标和教学特点，采用集群模块课程的教学方法，突出"宽基础、活模块"方式，使全套书内容既有系统性，又有相对的独立性，以适应各院校独自办学的特点。

第二，吸纳了当前旅游业先进的管理思想和经营理念，保证了本套教材的先进性与经营管理相结合的实践性。

第三，采用了国际上比较流行的教材结构，每一章都有必要的说明和提示，并将课外的相关知识、案例穿插在其中，以指导学生自学、明确目的，调动学生学习的积极性和主动性。

第四，本套教材不仅适用于高等院校旅游专业，其中大部分教材也适用于酒店管理专业。另外，也可以作为高等教育自学考试的教材和业内人士的自修参考书。

经过全体参编人员的共同努力,这套教材现已陆续出版,我们欢迎广大专家学者和教师批评指正。

在本套教材的编写过程中,得到了黑龙江省教育厅高教处的大力支持和明确指导,以及相关院校领导、专家学者和教师的帮助,在此,一并表示衷心的感谢!

编审委员会

2004 年 2 月

前　言

目前,我国旅游业正突飞猛进地向前发展,已经成为一大支柱产业。若要使其跟上时代发展的步伐,就要培养大批的旅游专业人才。

本书是为高等学校旅游专业学生编写的系列教材之一。参编人员都是从事多年旅游英语课程教学的一线教师。在编写时,尽量考虑不同层次学生的需求,尤其注意旅游专业学生的英语水平,做到内容由浅入深,词汇量适中,讲解详细。

本书由郭婷、艾治国任主编,张松、曹继宏、王艳滨、李佳玉任副主编。全书共分10个单元。每单元主要由精读、泛读和补充阅读材料三部分组成。内容主要分旅行英语和饭店英语两大部分。课文涉及旅游文化生活、旅游业发展、旅行社和航空公司的经营运作,以及宾馆接待服务、客房、餐饮等旅游工作人员常用知识等。每单元后的注释和常用句型采用中英文对照形式,练习紧紧围绕课文内容,使读者既提高了英语水平,又增加了旅游知识,实用性强。

本书既可作为高等学校旅游管理及相关专业的教材,也适合于旅游业人员自修、培训及英语专业学生泛读使用。

在本书的编写过程中,参考并借鉴了大量的相关教材,在此我们向有关作者表示感谢。完稿后,承蒙翟志群、葛洪久、艾厚新和杨秀姗教授的审读,在此也表示由衷的谢意。

由于时间仓促,加之水平有限,疏漏与不足之处在所难免,敬请广大读者批评指正。

编　者
2008年3月

Content

Unit 1　Flight Ticket Reservation ··· 1
　Text A: Air Travel ·· 1
　Dialogues ··· 2
　Exercises ··· 5
　Text B: The Airlines ··· 9
　Text C: Other Means of Transportation ··· 10
Unit 2　The Customs ·· 12
　Text A: At the Customs ·· 12
　Dialogues ·· 14
　Exercises ·· 17
　Text B: Passport and Visa ·· 21
　Text C: Customs Inspection ·· 22
Unit 3　Recreational Activities ··· 24
　Text A: Modern Life ·· 24
　Dialogue ··· 26
　Exercises ·· 29
　Text B: Traditional Chinese Festivals ··· 34
　Text C: Holidays in the U.S. ··· 37
Unit 4　Post Office ··· 40
　Text A: Postal and Telephone Services ··· 40
　Dialogues ·· 41
　Exercises ·· 44
　Text B: How did Stamps Come into Use ·· 50
　Text C: Modern Communication ·· 51
Unit 5　Hotel Services ··· 53
　Text A: Hotel Services ·· 53
　Dialogues ·· 55
　Exercises ·· 60
　Text B: Housekeeping Development ··· 66
　Text C: The Small Country Inn ·· 68

Unit 6　Home Away From Home ……… 71
Text A: Home Away From Home ……… 71
Dialogues ……… 73
Exercises ……… 77
Text B: The International Hotel Chains ……… 81
Text C: The Cashier ……… 86

Unit 7　Typical Chinese Cuisine ……… 90
Text A: Chinese Cuisine ……… 90
Dialogues ……… 94
Exercises ……… 96
Text B: Different Table Manners between Chinese and Westerners ……… 100
Text C: How to Cook Mapo Beancurd ……… 102

Unit 8　Chinese Tea ……… 104
Text A: Chinese Tea ……… 104
Dialogues ……… 107
Exercises ……… 109
Text B: Public Houses ……… 113
Text C: Tibetan Buttered Tea and Mongolian Milk Tea ……… 114

Unit 9　Sightseeing ……… 117
Text A: Reasons for People to Travel ……… 117
Dialogues ……… 119
Exercises ……… 123
Text B: The Travel Agency ……… 129
Text C: Thomas Cook ……… 131

Unit 10　Tourist Shopping ……… 133
Text A: Tourist Commodities ……… 133
Dialogues ……… 135
Exercises ……… 138
Text B: Chinese Carpets ……… 143
Text C: How to Develop New Tourist Commodities ……… 145

APPENDIX 1　Key to the Exercises ……… 147
APPENDIX 2　Chinese Translation of Texts A (Unit 1 ~ Unit 10) ……… 162
APPENDIX 3　Glossary ……… 182
APPENDIX 4　International Airlines ……… 193
APPENDIX 5　Hotel Organizations Chart ……… 195
APPENDIX 6　Chinese Scenic Spots ……… 198

Unit 1 Flight Ticket Reservation

Study structure
Text A (Intensive Reading): Air Travel
Dialogues
New Words and Expressions
Exercises
Text B (Extensive Reading): The Airlines
Text C (Supplementary Reading): Other Means of Transportation

Summary of the Text

　　Air travel is closely connected with airplanes with rapid development of the airline industry. Besides air travel, many other means of transportation provide tourists with more options.

Text A Air Travel

　　Airplane has become very common for long distance travel. Now, more and more people would like to take airplanes on their trips because air travel is fast and quite safe. Airlines have great influence on the service of air travel in many respects.

　　An airline, especially an international one, is a huge organization with many complex functions. There are tickets and reservations agents, airport passenger service personnel, cargo personnel, mechanics, catering service personnel, the flight crew, the flight service crew and so on.

　　The captain, or pilot, is in charge of the whole flight from start to finish, just like the captain of a ship. He is helped by the first officer who is second in command. There is also a pilot and flight engineer who is responsible for the functioning of all mechanics equipment. In the case of long-range flights, there may be an additional pilot, called a second officer. The flight crew performs its functions in the cockpit of the plane. Therefore, the passengers hardly see this part of the crew, though the captain may speak to them over the loudspeaker system. He usually says hello to them soon after takeoff and then gives them information about geographic places of interest and weather conditions during the flight.

For half a century, the job of an air hostess has been an exciting, stimulating and rewarding career. Although it is generally thought of in terms of women, it is by no means limited to them. Men play an important role in the ever-growing field, too.

For the crew, there is much to do to prepare for the flight even before they board the airplane. After arriving at the airport and signing in for work, they meet the other members of the crew and attend a briefing held by the captain. At this time, he mentions the flight plan, weather conditions, and other factors that might affect the meal service. About half an hour before departure, the passengers begin boarding the airplane and the cabin crew welcome them on board and help them find their seats. There are welcoming and other pre-takeoff announcements, as well as the emergency equipment demonstration. The last thing the air hostesses do before takeoff is to check the passengers' seat belts.

The role of the cabin crew becomes very busy once the airplane is airborne. It consists mainly of providing the passengers with food and drinks and involves a lot of work and attention to detail. When the flight nears its destination, the purser makes the announcements concerning landing procedures, and the cabin crew check to see if the passengers and the cabin are prepared for landing. After landing, they help the passengers disembark and say good-bye to them.

Dialogues: Booking Flight Tickets

Dialogue A

A: Good morning, American Airlines, Miss Mary's speaking. Can I help you?

B: Yes, I'd like to make a reservation to New York on June 6th, the day after tomorrow.

A: Hang on, please. Let me check for you. (A moment later) Thank you for waiting. I'm sorry but our flights are fully booked on that day. The next available flight leaves at 8 a.m., Sunday, June 7th. Shall I reserve you a seat then?

B: Yes, please.

Dialogue B

A: Hello, Air Canada. May I help you?

B: Yes, I'd like to get a ticket.

A: Would you prefer first class or economy?

B: Economy, please.

A: You may buy your ticket at any of our offices. Thank you for calling Air Canada.

B: Thank you.

Dialogue C

A: I'd like to cancel my reservation on Flight 125 to Beijing on the 3rd. My name is Tony Simpson.

B: Just a moment, please. Thank you for waiting. I've cancelled your reservation. Shall I make another reservation for you?

A: No, thanks.

B: I see. Please call us again for any further reservation. Thank you for calling British Airways.

New Words and Expressions

1. influence /ˈinfluəns/ n./v. 影响
2. aspect /ˈæspekt/ n. 方面
3. especially /iˈspeʃəli/ adv. 特别地，尤其
4. organization /ˌɔːgənaiˈzeiʃən/ n. 组织，机构
5. complex /ˈkɔmpleks/ adj. 复杂的
6. function /ˈfʌŋkʃən/ n. 功能，作用
7. reservation /ˌrezəˈveiʃən/ n. 预订
8. personnel /ˌpəːsəˈnel/ n. 人员，员工
9. cargo /ˈkɑːgəu/ n. 货物
10. mechanic /miˈkænik/ n. 机械工，技工
11. catering /ˈkeitəriŋ/ n. 公共饮食业；给养
12. crew /kruː/ n. 全体人员
13. in the case of 在……的情况
14. perform /pəˈfɔːm/ v. 履行，执行
15. cockpit /ˈkɔkpit/ n. 驾驶员座舱
16. loudspeaker /ˌlaudˈspiːkə/ n. 扬声器
17. geographic /ˌdʒiəˈgræfik/ adj. 地理学的，地理的
18. air hostess /ɛə//ˈhəustis/ n. 空姐

19. stimulating /'stimjuleitiŋ/ adj. 刺激的，有刺激性的
20. rewarding /ri'wɔ:diŋ/ adj. 报答的，有益的，值得的
21. in terms of 根据，按照，用……的话，在……方面
22. by no means 决不
23. play an important role in 在……中起重要作用
24. sign in 签到，记录到达时间，签收
25. briefing /'bri:fiŋ/ n. 情况介绍，简报
26. departure /di'pa:tʃə/ n. 启程，离开
27. cabin /'kæbin/ n. 小屋，机舱
28. announcement /ə'naunsmənt/ n. 宣告，发表
29. as well as 也，又
30. emergency /i'mə:dʒənsi/ n. 紧急情况，突然事件
31. equipment /i'kwipmənt/ n. 装备，器材
32. demonstration /'deməns'treiʃən/ n. 示范
33. seat belt 座椅安全带
34. consist of 由……组成
35. mainly /'meinli/ adv. 大体上，主要地
36. attention to 对……注意
37. destination /'desti'neiʃən/ n. 目的地
38. purser /'pə:sə/ n. 事务长
39. concerning /kən'sə:niŋ/ prep. 关于
40. procedure /prə'si:dʒə/ n. 程序，手续
41. disembark /ˌdisim'ba:k/ v. (使)起岸，(使)登陆
42. hang on 不挂断，稍等
43. available /ə'veiləbl/ adj. 可得到的，可利用的，有空的
44. prefer /pri'fɔ:/ v. 更喜欢，宁愿
45. first class 一流的，头等舱
46. economy /i'kɔnəmi/ n. 经济，节约，经济舱
47. cancel /'kænsəl/ v. 取消

Notes

1. He is helped by the first officer who is second in command.
   他的助手是副驾驶员，也就是第二指挥员。

2. There is also a pilot and flight engineer who is responsible for the functioning of all mechanics equipment.

还有一位飞行员,同时也是飞机工程师,他负责所有机械设备的正常运转。

3. Although it is generally thought of in terms of women, it is by no means limited to them.
虽然这一职业通常被认为是由女性来从事的,但决不仅限于她们。

4. The role of the cabin crew becomes very busy once the airplane is airborne.
飞机一起飞,机舱内的服务人员就开始忙碌起来。

5. When the flight nears its destination, the purser makes the announcements concerning landing procedures, and the cabin crew check to see if the passengers and the cabin are prepared for landing.
当飞机即将抵达目的地时,飞机事务长就会通知有关着陆程序,而机舱内的服务人员则开始检查乘客和机舱,为着陆作准备。

Useful Expressions and Patterns

1. 预订机票:
1) I'd like to make a reservation to...
2) I'd like to get a ticket on a flight to...
2. 取消预订:
I'd like to cancel my reservation on Flight...to...on...

Exercises

I. Answer the following questions according to Text A.

1. What are the main complex functions of an international airline?
2. What is the task of the flight engineer?
3. Can the passengers usually see the pilot? And how does the pilot contact them?
4. What does the captain advise the crew at the briefing before departure?
5. What are the cabin crew busy with when the airplane is airborne?

II. Mark the following statements with "T" (True) or "F" (False) according to Text A.

1. The captain, or pilot, is in charge of the functioning of all mechanical equipment, just like the captain of a ship.
2. The job of air hostess is always limited to women.
3. At the briefing the captain mentions the flight plan and weather conditions.
4. The first thing the air hostesses do before the airplane takes off is to check the

passengers' seat belts.

5. The cabin crew is not so busy after takeoff as before takeoff.

III. Translation.

1. Translate the following sentences into Chinese.

1) Since the United States is such an enormous country, traveling by plane is the only sensible way to tour the country if you want to visit most of the 50 States.

2) Air travel is cheaper, service is frequent and connections speedy.

3) On domestic flights, if you have your ticket and a reservation, all you need to do is to be at the airport an hour before flight time.

4) Airlines employ the largest number of workers at most commercial airports, and most of their employees work in the terminal buildings.

5) Most airlines have computer systems that quickly print tickets and check for vacancies on flights.

2. Translate the following sentences into English.

1) 您想预订哪天、哪次航班的机票？

2) 从这里到北京的航班每隔两小时一班。

3) 请记得确认一下您的航班。

4) 从纽约到上海的经济舱单程票是 800 美元。

5) 请在起飞前 1 小时到达机场。

IV. Complete the following dialogues.

1. A: Can I see _____ （国内航班时刻表）?

   B: Sure. _____ （给您）.

   A: You have three flights to Las Vegas?

   B: Yes, we do. We have had that service since last month. _____ （仅仅需要一小时） from Chicago.

2. A: I used to drive and it took me more than 6 hours one-way. _____ （票价多少钱）?

   B: $ 500 one-way.

   A: Counting _____, _____ （汽油、过桥费）, meals, and everything, it's rather cheap to fly. Let me have _____ （一张到天津的往返票）.

3. A: Do you have any _____ （直飞的航班）?

   B: Sorry, we don't. I don't think you can find any airlines which offer a non-stop flight to Tokyo

   A: OK. Thanks a lot.

   B: _____ （不用谢）.

4. A: Good afternoon, American Airlines. _____ （国内航班预订）. Can I help you?

   B: Yes, I'd like to _____ （一张明天到海口的机票）.

   A: We have flights to Haikou every two hours from 9:00 a.m. to 9:00 p.m., so you don't need a reservation. Seats are available on a "_____ （先到先供应）" basis.

   B: Oh, that's very convenient.

V. Vocabulary and Structure.

1. Fill in the blank with the words or expressions given below. Change the forms where necessary.

additional, briefing, reservations, rewarding, airborne, crew, demonstration, board, complex, function

   1) What he said was too _____ for me to understand.
   2) The _____ of a hammer is to hit nails into wood.
   3) It will take an _____ two weeks to finish the work.
   4) Mr. Bush gave an off-the-record press _____.
   5) A tour of the harbor is an immensely _____ experience.
   6) Please _____ your flight through the gate marked 6.
   7) Would you like me to give you a _____?
   8) Would you please get me air _____ for travel within China?
   9) We have been _____ for four hours.
   10) All sixty-eight passengers and _____ members were killed in the air crash.

2. Match the following two columns.

   A. boarding pass   a. 座椅安全带
   B. tourist card   b. 行李认领牌
   C. passport   c. 护照
   D. flight coupon   d. 登机牌
   E. claim tag   e. 旅行卡
   F. seat belt   f. 联运机票

3. Multiple Choices.

   1) Even though he has lived in China for many years, Mark still can not _____ himself to the Chinese customs.

       A. adopt   B. adjust   C. adapt   D. accept

   2) Since he often travels on business, he can _____ himself to sleeping in any place he can find.

    A. make   B. accustom   C. force   D. let

3) Mary has never been _____ a ship.

    A. abroad   B. aboard   C. above   D. absorb

4) What time is the mail _____ on Saturday?

    A. objected   B. outlet   C. delivered   D. starved

5) You don't have to pay any _____ on personal belongings.

    A. price   B. duty   C. expense   D. elevator

VI. Situational Dialogue.

Make up a dialogue according to the given situation:

An American trade delegation is invited to attend the Harbin Trade Fair by your company. You go to the airport to meet them on behalf of your company.

VII. Mini Dialogues.

Dialogue A

A: Excuse me. Are you Mr. Smith from America?

B: No, I'm afraid you've made a mistake. My name is Robinson. I have just got off the plane.

A: I'm sorry. I've got the wrong person.

B: Never mind.

A: But can you point out Mr. John Smith to me? He has just arrived from New York.

B: I think I can. See that man over there? He's Mr. Smith. He and I came by the same airplane.

A: Thank you so much.

Dialogue B

A: Excuse me; you must be Mr. Smith from America.

B: Yes, I'm John Smith from New York.

A: Nice to meet you. My name is Wang Lei. I'm from Fengda Corporation.

B: Nice to meet you, too, Mr. Wang.

A: Welcome to China, Mr. Smith. Our manager has asked me to come and meet you.

B: Thank you, Mr. Wang.

A: I hope you had a good trip.

B: Fine. I had a very pleasant flight.

A: I'm very glad to hear that. Let's take a short rest in the waiting room and then we are going through the formalities.

B: OK.

VIII. Practical Writing.

Reread Text A and write a working plan of the captain at a briefing before takeoff.

Text B The Airlines

Many different airlines have counters in the terminal building. The country's airline is not the only one that serves the airport. The country wants people from all over the world to come as tourists. Yet it can't afford to provide services everywhere. No one country or company can do this. Therefore, many different airlines provide service to and from the many different places people need or want to travel.

In addition, places visited by many travelers need to be served by more than one airline so that the passengers can have a wider choice of flights. There is so much competition among airlines for passengers that there are many different kinds of service available as well as different types and sizes of aircraft.

Since there are so many places that need airline service, there are many different routes. Besides that, because there are so many passengers for certain places, many of the trunk lines fly the same routes. To avoid confusion and air traffic problems, all airline routes are controlled either by local government or by international regulations. Airlines are regulated as to the number of flights, and many other things, by agreements between different countries or by government regulations.

The International Air Transport Association (IATA) is a voluntary association of international airlines that sets routes, fares and other standards of service. Most international airlines are members of the IATA. They decide things by agreement among themselves. Government influence, however, is very strong because many of the airlines are owned by governments.

Special government agencies regulate domestic airlines and those that fly into a country from other countries. The largest of these government agencies is the Civil Aeronautics Board (CAB) of the United States. Its function is to regulate and promote transportation within the country and between the United States and other countries. Even when they concern domestic flights, the decision of the CAB can have much influence throughout the world because of the importance of the United States to international tourism.

The CAB regulations not only benefit the airlines but also protect the passengers. There are regulations and standards for repairing and maintaining the aircraft. There are rules and measurements for training the people who fly, the people who take care of the aircraft or the passengers, and the people who operate the airports. Regulations concerning the safety of the aircraft and the passengers are most important.

Notes

1. International Air Transport Association (IATA) 国际航空运输协会
2. Civil Aeronautics Board 民用航空董事会

Exercises: Mark the following questions with "T" (True) or "False" (False) according to Text B

1. The country's airline doesn't only serve the airport.
2. There are many different airplane routes just because lots of places need airline service.
3. Local government control airlines routes in order to avoid confusion and air traffic problems.
4. The International Air Transport Association (IATA) is an official association of international airlines that sets routes, fares and other standards of service.
5. The CAB regulations are beneficial for the airlines.

Text C Other Means of Transportation

Being in a different place from one's usual residence is an essential feature of tourism. It means that transportation is one vital aspect in the tourism industry. Without the modern high-speed and inexpensive forms of transportation that are available to large numbers of people, tourism would be possible only for a tiny fraction of the population.

For many years, railroads have formed the first successful system of mass transportation, carrying crowds of tourists from one place to another. However, the automobile has now replaced the railroads for most local travels, especially in the United States. The automobile offers convenience. The traveler can depart from his own home and arrive at his destination without transferring luggage or having to cope with any other difficulties. Nowadays buses have partly replaced railroad passenger service on many local routes in a number of cities. However, railroad transportation is still very popular in China for internal travels.

  Ships still play an important part in tourism. A cruise is a voyage by ship that is made for pleasure rather than a voyage for a fixed destination. The cruise ship serves as the hotel for the passengers as well as their transportation. When the tourists reach a port, they are usually conducted on a one-day excursion, but they return to the ship to eat and sleep. The ship is no longer simply a means of transportation but a destination in itself.

  Subways are mostly found in large cities, such as New York, London and Paris. The subway is an underground system of high-speed trains. Subway trains move more quickly and efficiently than buses and they will deliver you to within walking distance of almost any place in the city. Taxis are another common means of transportation in most cities in the world. This kind of service does not have regular schedules so as to meet the needs of some individuals. If you are not familiar with a city, taxis are an extremely convenient way for you to get around. They are an essential link between the railroad station or airport and your destination in almost every city.

  Transportation services and facilities are an integral component of tourism. In fact, the success of practically all forms of travel depends on adequate transportation. And the increase in almost all forms of tourism boosts passenger traffic.

Notes

1. play an important part in... 在……中起重要作用
2. a cruise ship 游船

Exercises: Answer the following questions.

1. Why are transportation companies a vital aspect of the tourism industry?
2. What convenience does the automobile offer compared with the railroad?
3. What are the advantages of taxi and subway compared with the other means of transportation?
4. What does the success of practically all forms of travel rely on?

Unit 2　The Customs

Study structure
Text A (Intensive Reading): At the Customs
Dialogues
New Words and Expressions
Exercises
Text B (Extensive Reading): Passport and Visa
Text C (Supplementary Reading): Customs Inspection

Summary of the Text

　　To avoid trouble, the immigration rules and customs regulations must be observed. Generally speaking, it would be a good idea for tourists to know as much as possible about the country they are leaving for.

Text A　At the Customs

　　As the passengers leave the large airplane, Mary and John step forward to greet them. They are passenger service agents and represent their country's airline. They take care of passengers.

　　"Welcome," says John, "we're very happy to have you visit our county. If you will please follow us, we'll take you to the immigration area."

　　The deplaning passengers follow the passenger service agents into the large terminal building.

　　In the terminal building are the immigration, customs, and baggage areas, as well as ticket and reservation desks for many airlines.

　　There are also waiting rooms, shops, restaurants, and other facilities for the traveler's comfort.

　　"Will immigration take long?" Mrs. Clinton asks as they follow Mary through the long hallway in the terminal.

　　"I don't think so," answers Mary, "there are many immigration officials.

They try to take care of tourists as quickly as possible."

"Good," says Mr. Clinton, "we're all tired of being stuck in the plane. We're eager to get started seeing your country."

As the passengers enter the immigration area, they see people lined up in front of high counters. An immigration officer sits behind each counter. Hanging from the ceiling over one group of counters is a large sign reading: Tourists-Visitors. Mary directs the Clintons to that section.

"It shouldn't take very long," she tells them as they get on line. "Please be sure to have your immigration information cards and your passports or other documents ready. I hope you'll enjoy your stay in our country."

A document is an official paper. A passport is a document that gives a person permission to leave and then re-enter a country. A country issues passports to its own citizens. Mr. Clinton has one passport from his country for himself and his wife.

In the immigration area, the passenger agents answer questions and help the people waiting in line. Some people are returning to the country from trips to other places. They are either nationals or residents of the country.

Although "immigrate" means coming into a country with the intention to live there, all persons entering a country must go through immigration, no matter how short their stay will be.

Their documents and identification must be checked by an immigration official. In this way, a country keeps track of the people entering and knows the countries from which tourists and visitors come. Tourists and other visitors must fill out the immigration information cards to explain their purpose for entering the country.

People who intend to stay in a country permanently are called immigrants. Sometimes they are married to nationals or citizens of the country. They may wish to live in the country but keep their own citizenship. Other people intend to become citizens of the country after they live there a certain length of time. All immigrants must have special documents that explain their intentions.

Often people who wish to remain permanently in a country must be recommended by a citizen of that country. The citizen must be responsible for the immigrant. The citizen promises that the immigrant will not be a burden on the country. The citizen also assures the country that the immigrant is not a criminal escaping from another country.

It takes longer for immigrants and returning nationals or residents to go through immigration. That is why there are usually separate lines for each group. However, the officials are anxious to let visitors go through immigration as quickly and easily as possible.

Dialogues: Going through the Customs

Dialogue A

A: May I see your passport, please?

B: Of course. Here you are.

A: How long will you stay in New York?

B: For about a month.

A: Do you have anything to declare?

B: Yes. I bought a watch and a new suit.

A: You're allowed $100 duty-free, so you don't have to pay any duty on your watch and suit.

B: Thank you, sir.

Dialogue B

A: Could you put that suitcase on the counter and open it, please? What's inside?

B: A package of green tea and some bananas.

A: I'm sorry, sir. You are not supposed to bring fresh fruits into the United States. I'm going to confiscate them.

B: Oh, that's too bad.

Dialogue C

A: How long do you plan to stay?

B: About a month.

A: And what's the purpose of your trip?

B: I'm going to visit my friends.

A: Let's take a look at this bag. Can you open it?

B: Sure.

A: Is this camera a gift for someone?

B: No, it's my camera for personal use.

New Words and Expressions

1. agent /'eidʒənt/ n. 代理人,代理商
2. represent /ˌriːpriˈzent/ v. 代表

第 2 单元 海关

3. immigration /ˌimiˈgreiʃən/ — n. 外来的移民，移居入境
4. deplane /ˌdiˈplein/ — v. 下飞机
5. terminal /ˈtəːminl/ — n. 终点站，终端; adj. 末期
6. customs /ˈkʌstəmz/ — n. 海关
7. baggage /ˈbægidʒ/ — n. 行李
8. facility /fəˈsiliti/ — n. 设备，工具
9. comfort /ˈkʌmfət/ — n. 舒适
10. hallway /ˈhɔːlwei/ — n. 走廊
11. be tired of — 厌烦
12. stick(stuck, stuck) /stik/ — v. 固定，粘住
13. ceiling /ˈsiːliŋ/ — n. 天花板
14. sign /sain/ — n. 标记，符号
15. direct /diˈrekt/ — v. 指引，指向
16. section /ˈsekʃən/ — n. 部分，区
17. document /ˈdɔkjumənt/ — n. 文件，文献
18. permission /pəˈmiʃən/ — n. 许可
19. issue /ˈisjuː/ — v. 发放，发行
20. citizen /ˈsitizn/ — n. 市民，公民
21. resident /ˈrezidənt/ — n. 居民
22. immigrate /ˈimigreit/ — v. 使移居入境，移来
23. identification /aiˌdentifiˈkeiʃən/ — n. 身份证明，识别
24. check /tʃek/ — v. 检查
25. keep track of — 明了
26. fill out — 填写
27. purpose /ˈpəːpəs/ — n. 目的，意图
28. permanently /ˈpəːməntli/ — adv. 永久地
29. citizenship /ˈsitizənʃip/ — n. 公民身份
30. intend /inˈtend/ — v. 想要，打算
31. length /leŋθ/ — n. 长度
32. special /ˈspeʃəl/ — adj. 特别的
33. intention /inˈtenʃən/ — n. 意图，目的
34. recommend /rekəˈmend/ — v. 推荐，介绍
35. promise /ˈprɔmis/ — v./n. 许诺，答应
36. burden /ˈbəːdn/ — n. 负担

37. assure /əˈʃuə/ v. 保证
38. escape /isˈkeip/ v. 逃脱
39. separate /ˈsepərit/ adj. 单独的
40. anxious /ˈæŋkʃəs/ adj. 渴望的
41. suit /sjuːt/ n. 一套衣服
42. duty-free /ˈdjuːtiˈfriː/ adj. 免税的
43. package /ˈpækidʒ/ n. 包裹，包
44. confiscate /ˈkɔnfiskeit/ v. 没收

Notes

1. immigration area 入境处；immigration office 移民局；immigration official 移民官。

2. If you will please follow us, we'll take you to the immigration area. 在 if 引导的从句中，will 是作为情态动词使用的，表示一种意愿。

3. the terminal building 意为航空集散大楼。一般来讲，机场有一个或多个集散大楼。其内部设有候机厅、商店、餐馆和其他一些为乘客提供便利服务的设施。

4. as...as possible 意为尽可能地……。例如，as quickly as possible, as easily as possible.

5. be tire of 同义的词组还有 be fed up with, 意为厌烦。例如，I'm tired of watching TV at home and let's go out for a walk. 我厌倦了在家里看电视，让我们出去走走吧。

6. be eager to 意为急切，渴望。例如，The company is eager to expand into new markets. 公司急欲开辟新市场。

7. either...or... 意为不是……就是……。例如，It's either blue, red, or green—I can't remember. 不是蓝色的，就是红色的，要不就是绿色的，我记不清了。

8. no matter how 意为不管如何。例如，No matter how long it takes, I'll finish the job on time. 不管花多长时间，我都要按时完成工作。

Useful Expressions and Patterns

1. Do you have any restrictions on...?
你们对……有限制吗？
Do you have any restrictions on the articles we're carrying at the customs?
你们对我们随身携带的物品在过海关的时候有限制吗？

2. Your personal belongs are not dutiable.
   你的个人物品不上税。
3. Do you have anything to declare? 你有什么要申报的吗?
4. Do I have to pay duty on...?
   我得给……上税吗?
   Do I have to pay duty on the liquor and cigarettes?
   我得给酒和香烟上税吗?

Exercises

I. Answer the following questions according to Text A.
1. What is the job of the passenger service agents?
2. What is a terminal building?
3. Please explain the following terms: document, passport and immigrate.
4. According to the text, what do people usually do if they want to live permanently in a foreign country?

II. Mark the following statements with "T" (True) or "F" (False) according to Text A.
1. Passenger service agents act for their country's airline. They serve passengers.
2. There are waiting rooms, stores, fast-food restaurants, cinemas, hospitals and schools in the terminal building.
3. Passports can be issued to foreign citizens by China.
4. Sometimes an immigration official doesn't have to check every passenger's documents and identification.
5. People who intend to stay in a foreign country permanently are called citizens.

III. Translation.
1. Translate the following sentences into Chinese.
1) As the passengers leave the large airplane, Mary and John step forward to greet them.
2) In the terminal building are the immigration, customs, and baggage areas, as well as ticket and reservation desks for many airlines.
3) They try to take care of tourists as quickly as possible.
4) Please be sure to have your immigration information cards and your passports or other documents ready.
5) Tourists and other visitors must fill out the immigration information cards to

explain their purpose for entering the country.

2. Translate the following sentences into English.

　　1) 先生,您有什么要申报的吗?

　　2) 对不起,先生。这件东西你得付进口关税。

　　3) 祝您在北京过得愉快!

　　4) 请您把那个提包放到柜台上打开好吗?

　　5) 你计划在上海呆多久?

IV. Complete the following dialogues.

A: _____(您的护照), please?

B: Wait a moment, please. It's in the purse. Here it is.

A: _____(您有什么要申报的吗)?

B: I'm not sure. I have some gifts for my friends.

A: What are they?

B: _____(几瓶香水和威士忌酒).

A: Oh, that's more than we can allow you free.

B: All right.

A: Now, would you please _____(打开您的手提包以便检查)?

B: Yes, please.

A: I'm afraid these books are not prohibited entry.

B: _____(我该如何处理这些书)?

A: You can leave them at our checkroom and pick them up when you leave China.

B: OK.

A: The rest is fine. And please _____(填写外币申报表).

B: Sure. How much do I have to pay for my duty?

A: I'll let you know in a minute. It's a 25 dollars altogether.

V. Vocabulary and Structure.

1. Fill in the blank with the words or expressions given below. Change the forms where necessary.

out of style, influence, fortune, host, salary, in advance, custom, honest, tone, overnight

1) The _____ of the dinner party was disappointed at the small number of guests who attended.

2) The _____ of the teacher's voice was gentle but authoritative.

3) The _____ of having one's marriage arranged by parents has disappeared in many parts of the world but continues in some Asian and African countries.

4) I don't want to _____ you. You must act on your own judgment.
5) Though the job requires a great deal of effort, the _____ is quite slow.
6) As far as I'm concerned, some days are lucky while others seem marked by bad _____.
7) He was a _____ person in spite of his great success.
8) We should make our reservations as far _____ as possible to get the flight we want.
9) I'll have my long skirts shortened because they are _____ now.
10) We took a(an) _____ train to Paris, which arrived just as the sun rose.

2. Match the following two columns.

A. represent   a. person who is a citizen of a country
B. deplane   b. person who lives in a country but may be a citizen of another country
C. agent   c. official document that gives a person permission to leave and reenter a country
D. passport   d. act for
E. resident   e. leave an airplane
F. immigrant   f. person who acts for another person or company
G. national   g. person planning to stay in a country permanently

3. Multiple Choices.

1) He _____ his father in appearance but not in height.
   A. repeats   B. looks   C. resembles   D. likes
2) The airplane took off soon. It was like being on an old train _____ from side to side and going faster and faster.
   A. surrounding B. foregoing   C. swaying   D. frowning
3) When he caught a _____ of his girl-friend in the rain, Jack asked the taxi driver to stop to pick her up.
   A. harbor   B. kettle   C. glimpse   D. scale
4) He always _____ to everything and never agrees with anybody.
   A. projects   B. gives   C. folds   D. objects
5) Smoking and drinking are regarded as _____ in some countries because they do no good to health.
   A. vices   B. habits   C. customs   D. copies
6) It is highly _____ that he come here tomorrow to join us.
   A. desirable   B. doubtful   C. good   D. wanted

7) If you just stay in this city for few days, we can give you a _____ library card and you can still make use of the books in the city library.

   A. terminal　　　B. temporary　　　C. regular　　　D. chamber

8) These programs are designed for those young people who want to _____ higher education but do not have enough time to go to university.

   A. insure　　　B. purse　　　C. purchase　　　D. pursue

9) I have not heard anything from him since his _____.

   A. departure　　　B. fault　　　C. foundation　　　D. acceptance

10) In order to increase our output, we need to import more production _____.

    A. facilities　　　B. hens　　　C. votes　　　D. artists

VI. Situational Dialogue.

Make up a dialogue according to the given situation:

You are an overseas Chinese coming back to visit your relatives and bring with you some presents for them. Now you are going through the customs formalities.

VII. Mini Dialogues.

Dialogue A

A: Have you got anything to declare, sir?

B: I don't know. You see, this is my first trip to China and I'm not quite sure about the procedure here.

A: Well, have you gone through the immigration office?

B: Yes, I have done that.

A: And the quarantine inspection?

B: Yes.

A: Very well. Have you filled in the customs declaration form?

B: Only partially. It looks rather complicated and I'm not sure how to fill it out.

A: I can help you. Please give me your passport and your declaration form. Now, what you need to do is simply look through the two lists, the Prohibited Articles List and the Duty-free Quota List. Right here.

Dialogue B

A: Now, Mr. Thompson, please give me your luggage check. I'll go and get your luggage.

B: Here you are, Mike. I have two suitcases.

A: Please wait here. I'll be right back.

(After a while, Mike returns.)

A: I'm terribly sorry, Mr. Thompson. The airport in New York made a mistake and put only one of your suitcases on your flight. The other suitcase is still in New York.

B: Oh, Jesus. What can I do?

A: I have contacted New York airport and they said they were awfully sorry and would put it on the next flight.

B: And when will it arrive here?

A: Seven o'clock this evening. The airport here will send the suitcase to your hotel.

B: Thank you very much.

VIII. Practical Writing.

Please refer to some relevant customs formalities and learn to fill out Customs Declaration Form.

Text B Passport and Visa

A passport is a travel document that identifies the holder as a citizen of the country. A passport also requests other countries to give the holder safe passage and all lawful aid and protection. Sometimes a passport must have a visa (official endorsement) from the country a person desires to visit before entry into that country is permitted.

Generally, the government issues three types of passports: (1) diplomatic, for people going abroad on important government assignments; (2) official, for other government employees; (3) regular, for people traveling overseas for personal reasons.

Many countries do not require citizens of certain other countries to have passports. United States citizens, for instance, do not need passports to enter Bermuda, Canada, Mexico and most of the West Indies.

A visa is an endorsement that government officials place on a passport to show that the passport is valid. Officials of the country a traveler is entering grant the visa. The visa certifies that the traveler's passport has been examined and approved. Immigration officers then permit the bearer to enter the country. A government that does not want a person to enter the country can refuse to grant that person a visa.

Notes

1. A passport also requests other countries to give the holder safe passage and all lawful aid and protection.
   护照还要求别国给其持有人以安全通过权并给予各种合法的帮助与保护。
2. Generally, the government issues three types of passports: diplomatic, official and regular.
   一般来说,政府签发三种护照:外交护照、公务护照和普通护照。
3. A visa is an endorsement that government officials place on a passport to show that the passport is valid.
   签证是政府官员在护照上签署的证明,以表明该护照有效。

Exercises: Answer the following questions.

1. What is the definition of a passport?
2. What are three types of passports issued by government?
3. Do all the countries require citizens of some other countries to have passports? If not, please give some examples.
4. What is the definition of a visa?
5. What is the function of a visa?

Text C Customs Inspection

Customs inspectors examine the baggage of all travelers to the country. All articles acquired abroad must be declared—that is, they must be identified and their value given to an inspector. If a person fails to declare an article or understates its value, the article may be taken away and the individual may be fined.

In the United States, articles totaling up to $400 are exempt (free from any duty) if they meet certain regulations. For example, the articles must be for personal use, and the person's trip must have lasted at least 48 hours. Also the articles cannot be prohibited or restricted by federal regulations. The $400 exemption can be claimed by a person once every 30 days. The 48-hour rule does not apply to trips to Mexico or the Virgin Islands.

If a traveler cannot claim the $400 exemption because of the 48-hour or 30-day restriction, he or she may claim a $25 exemption. However, a person must pay duties on all articles if their total value exceeds $25. Duty rates depend on the type, value, and quantity of the articles.

Notes

1. All articles acquired abroad must be declared—that is, they must be identified and their value given to an inspector.

   所有国外要求申报的物品必须申报——也就是说,它们必须被认定且必须向官员申报价值。

2. If a person fails to declare an article or understates its value, the article may be taken away and the individual may be fined.

   如果你没有申报某一物品或少报其价值,该物品可能被没收,而你则可能被罚款。

3. If a traveler cannot claim the $400 exemption because of the 48-hour or 30-day restriction, he or she may claim a $25 exemption.

   如果游客由于旅行48小时或30天的限制规定而不能享受400美元的免税,他(她)也可以享受25美元的免税。

Exercises: Mark the following questions with "T"(True) or "False"(False) according to Text C.

1. Customs inspectors examine the baggage of all suspicious travelers to the country.
2. Not all articles acquired abroad have to be declared.
3. If a person can't declare his article, the article might be confiscated.
4. In America, articles worth four hundred dollars are free from any duty if they meet certain regulations.
5. Duty rates vary in type, value and quantity of the articles.

Unit 3 Recreational Activities

Study Structure

Text A (Intensive Reading): Modern Life
Dialogues
New Words and Expressions
Exercises
Text B (Extensive Reading): Traditional Chinese Festivals
Text C (Supplementary Reading): Holidays in the U.S.

Summary of the Text

This unit mainly talks about modern life, which introduces how you should enjoy life. And then let you know some traditional Chinese festivals, such as, National Day, the Spring Festival, the Mid-Autumn Festival and so on. Moreover, you'll know holidays in the U.S. according to the calendar. I believe, after learning, you'll feel relaxed and enjoy really recreational activities.

Text A Modern Life

Nowadays the usual work time of a week in China is 40 hours. This gives our Chinese people more time for recreation, such as fishing, swimming, skiing, bowling, photography, gardening and so on, which are popular leisure pursuits.

A two-day weekend system or longer vacation for the Labor Day and the National Day can provide more time for people to do the things they like. Many Chinese use this time to travel, especially to see the magnificent scenery, natural wonders and places of historical interest which can be found in so many parts of the country. Each year millions of people visit different national parks, in many of which visitors can swim, go fishing, take part in all kinds of activities. There are a lot of recreational areas in China now. It's so good for people to relax from daily tiredness.

Traveling is a wonderful thing. But in the past, it seemed to be a distant thing. Now the young generation have a different life style. Traveling proves to be a good way to relieve strain. As we all know, Americans love to travel. Young

Americans would travel all the time if they had time and money. It is an adventure to be shared with friends. It can be to the Rocky Mountains, to Hawaii, to Florida and to Texas and New York. It all depends on what you want to do... climb mountains? Go surfing? Go horse-back riding? It all depends on your interests and your pocket-book. How much time do you have and how much money? Time and money are two major challenges, and those two factors will determine where you travel, when, and for how long.

Many American high-school and college students have to work part-time, if not full-time to go to school. This means that they usually work in the afternoons and evenings and weekends and during their vacations in order to save enough money for tuition, books, cars and clothes. Many middle-class Americans are unable to pay all the bills for their children so the children help by working. As the money is for school and not for travel, it is only when there is money left over (usually not much), that there is a chance to go somewhere not too far away. The time to travel is precious; therefore, if a student only has two weeks, he/she will have to plan ahead and buy a cheap ticket to a destination, which is affordable.

As a young man or woman we can do without a lot of food, a soft bed, a lot of money. We have health, which means strength, endurance and a positive outlook. We are also young, which gives you the freedom to find adventure and to enjoy it! When we travel, we open a book, and each page is filled with a voyage to another territory in your life. We can benefit from this by being open to experience... and joy.

There is a proverb "All work and no play makes Jack a dull boy", do you agree with it? In modern life, people need time to refresh themselves as machines do to be refueled. Neither our brains nor our muscles can do without sufficient relaxation, since both are inevitably worn out after a certain period of work. So sometimes one should stop working in order to continue to work and work better. Moreover, play can do us good in many ways. Play is one of the natural sources of human ability. Life experience is what one gets when he is playing, besides learning and working. In return, he applies his experience to his work.

In short, as modern people, we should live a modern life—work hard and enjoy a lot!

Dialogue: Chinese New Year's Day

Y = Yang   B = Bob

Y: Happy New Year, Bob!

B: I wish you a Happy New Year.

Y: How glad we are to have such fine weather!

B: Yes, it is just the right weather for New Year's Day.

Y: How will you spend the New Year's Day?

B: I want to go out and see how the street and people look.

Y: All shops are closed. Perhaps people are still sleeping. Chinese people are usually busy on New Year's Eve. Some of them don't sleep the whole night. When the morning comes they all feel tired. Then they go to bed.

B: What do you do that night?

Y: We watch TV, drink, dance, sing, play cards, worship and pray to different gods and many other things. Everything must be done before dawn.

B: What is on TV? Is there something special on?

Y: Yes, CCTV holds parties on New Year's Eve. The overseas Chinese can also watch this special program on TV.

B: Do you visit your friends?

Y: Yes, but New Year's visitors are decreasing, year after year. Sometimes, we just say "Happy New Year" to each other by phone or short messages.

B: Well, that may be true.

Y: Let's go out and see how the streets look today.

B: They look quite different from yesterday.

Y: Yes, everybody looks happy and cheerful. There are people running about making visits.

B: Look at the decoration of that bank. How beautiful!

Y: I think the New Year's decorations are getting more and more elaborate every year.

B: Without decorations, there would be no New Years.

Y: True. We feel somewhat lonelier when they are taken off.

B: It reminds us that time flies.

Y: When the holidays are over, we'll go back to work, fresh and energetic. We'll have a new beginning.

New words

1. recreation /ˌrekriˈeiʃn/ n. 娱乐，消遣
2. skiing /ˈskiːiŋ/ n. 滑雪
3. photography /fəˈtɔgrəfi/ n. 摄影术；照相术
4. leisure /ˈleʒə/ n. 空闲，闲暇
5. magnificent /mægˈnifisnt/ adj.（建筑物、景色等）雄伟的、壮丽的
6. scenery /ˈsiːnəri/ n. 景色，风景
7. generation /ˌdʒenəˈreiʃn/ n. 同时代的人们，一代
8. relieve /riˈliːv/ v. 解除，减轻
9. strain /strein/ n. 紧张，负担
10. adventure /ədˈventʃə/ n. 冒险
11. surf /sɔːf/ v. 参加冲浪运动
12. challenge /ˈtʃælindʒ/ n. 挑战
13. determine /diˈtəːmin/ v. 决心，决定
14. tuition /tjuːˈiʃn/ n.(大学、书院等的)学费
15. destination /ˌdestiˈneiʃn/ n.(旅行的)目的地，终点
16. affordable /əˈfɔːdəbl/ adj.能负担得起的
17. endurance /inˈdjuərəns/ n.忍耐，耐久力
18. positive /ˈpɔzətiv/ adj.积极的
19. outlook /ˈautluk/ n.展望，见解
20. voyage /ˈvɔiidʒ/ n.航海，航行
21. territory /ˈteritəri/ n.领域，范围
22. benefit /ˈbenifit/ v.(因……)得到利益
23. sufficient /səˈfiʃnt/ adj.充分的
24. inevitably /inˈevitəbli/ adv.不可避免地
25. moreover /mɔːˈrəuvə/ adv.并且，除此之外
26. source /sɔːs/ n.源头，根源
27. worship /ˈwəːʃip/ v.崇拜，敬仰
28. pray /prei/ v.祈祷
29. decrease /diˈkriːs/ v.使减少
30. cheerful /ˈtʃiəful/ adj. 快活的，愉快的
31. elaborate /iˈlæbərət/ adj.精致的，精心的
32. decoration /dekəˈreiʃn/ n.装饰
33. remind /riˈmaind/ v.提醒

第 3 单元 娱乐活动

34. energetic /enə'dʒetik/ adj. 精力充沛的

Notes

1. popular leisure pursuits 指大众的消遣活动。
2. the Labor Day 指五一劳动节,通常法定假日为三天,常采取串休的方式休息一周左右,以方便旅游。
3. the National Day 指十一国庆节,也是出游的最佳时间。
4. provide... for 供给(某人)……,也可用, provide... with。
5. places of historical interest 名胜古迹。
6. prove to be 证明……是。
7. the Rocky Mountains 落基山脉,是位于美国西部,北至阿拉斯加州,向南延伸至新墨西哥州的大山脉。
8. Hawaii 夏威夷岛,美国著名的旅游胜地。
9. depend on 依赖,取决于。
10. pocket-book 钱包,手提包。
11. part-time 兼职,非专任。
12. full-time 全部上班(工作)时间;专职,专任。
13. benefit... from 从……中获益。
14. All work and no play makes Jack a dull boy. 只会工作不会玩,使得杰克变得很愚钝。这是一句谚语,告诫人们要劳逸结合。
15. worship and pray to different gods 祭拜众神,祈求赐福,这是中国的传统,尤其对于老年人来说。
16. take off 取下,除去。

Useful Expressions and Patterns

祝福语句

1. Happy New Year to you!
   祝你新年快乐!
2. Merry Christmas to you!
   祝你圣诞快乐!
3. Have a good time!
   祝你愉快!
4. Have a nice trip!
   祝你旅途愉快!
5. You have my blessing!

我祝福你!

6. Happy landing!
   祝你一路顺风!

7. I sure enjoyed myself this evening.
   今天晚上我的确很快乐。

8. With best wishes for a happy new year.
   祝你新年快乐!

9. Our sincerest wishes for continued success.
   我们诚挚祝你继续成功。

10. May I wish you continued success and happiness in the long year to come.
    祝你永远成功快乐。

Exercises

Ⅰ. Answer the following questions according to Text A.

1. How many hours do the Chinese usually work for a week?
2. What can provide more time for people to the things they like?
3. What is good for people to relax from daily tiredness?
4. What can determine where to go and for how long?
5. Do you agree with "All work and no play makes Jack a dull boy"? Why?
6. What can you benefit from travel in the modern life?

Ⅱ. Mark the following statements with "T" (True) or "F" (False) according to Text A.

1. Each year only a few people visit national parks.
2. In the old days, people can't travel a lot.
3. Traveling proves to be a good way to reduce pressure.
4. Where to travel and for how long must depend on whether you have a small book for travel.
5. Many American students have to work all the time in order to save money for travel.
6. In order to work better, we can't stop until we finish the work, even though we are very tired.

Ⅲ. Translation.

1. Translate the following sentences into Chinese.

1) The automobile and the airplane in still more recent times have also become

major modes of transportation for recreational purposes.

2) But the new travelers could not have made their journeys without a dramatic decline of the cost of their undertaking—or without the Congress of Vienna, which laid the basis for a stable peace in which to admire the scenery.

3) Golden Ages are times of prosperity and achievement, but they are also eras of renewed values. The impending travel boom is liable to be the same.

4) In many countries, summer was the traditional vacation season. In the United States, for example, people went off to a resort in the mountains or at the seashore during the hot months.

5) A large number of sightseeing trips are part-day or one-day excursions to local points of interest.

2. Translate the following into English.

1)每年阴历正月初一是中国人的传统节日——春节,这是家人团聚的时刻。

2)节日也是举行婚礼的吉日良辰,因为大家都有足够的时间来庆祝。

3)在中秋之夜,家人团聚,赏月、品月饼,享受着家庭和睦的气氛。

4)泼水节是中国少数民族傣族的传统佳节。

5)农历九月九日是老人节,又称重阳节。全社会将开展一系列尊老爱老活动。

6)与世界上其他国家不一样的是,中国人既使用阳历,但同时也使用阴历(农历)。

Ⅳ. Complete the following dialogue.

You: Leo, this notice contains something interesting for you.

Leo: Oh? What is it _____?

You: It's for a training class, learning _____ cook Chinese dishes.

Leo: Hey, _____ exactly what my wife and I need.

You: Let me tell you all the _____.

Leo: Yes, please. _____ will it be?

You: It will be in the winter holiday for the Chinese _____.

Leo: We'd be free then. _____ be given in the company canteen?

You: You're right. The chef from _____ will be the chief instructor.

Leo: I love Sichuan food; it's so delicious! A bit too hot for my wife, though.

You: Here it says the chef is also _____ making desserts and snacks.

Leo: I can hardly wait. _____ Should we pay for the training?

You: Listen: "Price: A dish for the potluck dinner at _____ of the training!"

Leo: That sounds real fun. I'm _____ we'll enjoy the class.

You: And you could _____ with the same interest there.

Leo: I'll tell this to my wife. She'd be overjoyed to _____ .

Ⅴ. **Vocabulary and Structure.**

1. Fill in the blank with the words or expressions given below. Change the form where necessary.

   in turn, have...effect on, take care of, carry out, call upon, take on, in that sense, in addition, on occasion, be related to

   1) Training, a must for all hotel employees, _____ an added significance for the members of this staff.
   2) The resident manager _____ what may be the most important responsibility of the general manager.
   3) The director of sales is _____ to make more decisions affecting not only present but future earnings than any other department head.
   4) _____, the successful manager must implement and improve them and, _____ may be forced to completely disregard them.
   5) Note that the number of employees in a department _____ not _____ the classification of its department head.
   6) They are all members of the management team and, _____, equally important.
   7) Proper maintenance and provision of hotel services _____ a significant _____ the attitude of a guest toward the hotel.
   8) A general manager directly hired by the owner, selected the department heads, who _____ hired their own staffs.
   9) It is the employees who _____ the guests.

2. Match the following two columns.

   A. 休短假   a. modern tourism
   B. 轻松娱乐   b. the mode of travel
   C. 休闲时光   c. relax and have fun
   D. 旅行方式   d. leisure time
   E. 需求不足   e. a wilderness park
   F. 尽情享受旅游之快乐 f. need deficiencies
   G. 现代旅游   g. overseas Chinese
   H. 带薪假日   h. indulge in tourism
   I. 天然公园   i. paid holidays
   J. 海外华侨   j. take short-break holidays

3. Multiple Choices.

1) The executive housekeeper has the largest staff to supervise, yet reports to _____.

　　A. the resident manager　　　　B. the general manager

　　C. the personnel director　　　　D. the banquet manager

2) The personnel director's only responsibility is _____.

　　A. to report to the general manager

　　B. to staff the hotel

　　C. to make polices

　　D. to assist in running the hotel

3) The country from which the tourist comes is called _____ country.

　　A. destination　　　　B. origin

　　C. vacation　　　　　D. native

4) _____ is the name given to the business of serving tourists.

　　A. Accommodations　　B. Tourism

　　C. Travel　　　　　　D. Customs

5) No tours or activities are scheduled on _____ so the tourists can do whatever they like.

　　A. holidays　　　　B. free days

　　C. vacations　　　　D. timetables

Ⅵ. Situational Dialogue.

Make up a dialogue according to the given situation.

This is a dialogue between a couple. They have just married and are talking about where they can have a honey moon. At last, they decide to go to the south, such as, Hangzhou, Suzhou and Shanghai, etc.

Ⅶ. Mini Dialogue.

A: This one looks great! I love the seashore.

B: So do I. The sun... the sand... the ocean!

A: And listen to this! What do you think of sailing, swimming, windsurfing, and fishing?

B: Oh, Tom! They sound fantastic. I really like all those things.

A: Yeah...me, too.

B: Well, except fishing. To be honest, I hate fishing, but I love all the others.

A: Hey! Look at this! We can stay in a big hotel or we can stay in a little cabin by the beach.

B: You know, I really don't like those big hotels.

A: Neither do I. Let's stay in a cabin. It'll be much nicer right beside the ocean.

Ⅷ. Practical Writing.

圣诞贺卡和新年贺卡上通常印有祝词。祝词一般都已程式化。人们可视情况加些祝贺的话或其他内容，如"A Very Merry Christmas and a Very Happy New Year!"。祝词开头写对方的名字，如"To John"，最后写寄卡人的名字，如"From Marry"。To 与 From 可以省略。不过句中 Christmas 和 New Year 的首字母均需大写。

圣诞贺卡和新年贺卡的祝词在语言上有以下特点：

(1) 句首第一个字母大写,句中 Christmas 和 New Year 的首字母均需要大写。

(2) 通常为省略句型,如 "Sending you wishes for a beautiful Christmas and a New Year filled with happiness!" 此句句首省略了"I am"；两个名词短语以 "and" 连接成并列结构，如 "Season's Greetings and Best Wishes for the Coming Year!"；常为介词短语结构，如 "With warm wishes for every happiness throughout the season and in the New Year!"；也有分词短语结构，如 "Wishing you the many blessings of a Joyous Christmas and a Happy New Year!"

Simulated Writing.

1. Translate the following card into Chinese.

> Season's Greetings
> To Tina,
>   A wish for Peace and Happiness at this Christmas Season
>   From Joe

2. Translate the following card into Enylish.

> 亲爱的詹妮弗,
>   祝您
>   圣诞愉快,新年快乐
>   并祝您
>   2005年万事如意!
>   您真诚的朋友
>   小芳

Text B Traditional Chinese Festivals

China is a country with 56 peoples and a rich cultural heritage. Of all the traditional festivals, perhaps the following are the most popular ones in China.

National Day (October 1st) is the most important public festival in China as the anniversary of the founding of the People's Republic.

On this day, in large cities, people throng the streets, squares and parks in their holiday best. Main streets and public buildings are decorated with flags and flowers. In the evening these places are a blaze of light. Fireworks shooting, singing and dancing, various assemblies and exhibitions keep the whole nation busy for days.

The festivals next in importance after National Day are two New Years; one according to the Gregorian solar calendar, and the other according to the traditional lunar calendar. The former was officially established in 1911, but it has been to this day the New Year in an administrative sense only. Whereas the traditional New Year has remained the virtual festival of new year emotionally and culturally, though it was renamed "the Spring Festival" long ago.

The Spring Festival is the festival of festivals, which is deep-rooted in the life and soul of hundreds of hundreds of millions of people. It is a time of family reunion, good wishes, thanksgiving, new promises, hopes for the future, and merrymaking. Although officially there are only three full days, the celebrations of the Spring Festival take place in late January or early February and last for nearly a month, beginning ten days before the end of the New Year. The historical reason for beginning the year during cold weather is that it is a time between the "autumn harvest and winter storage" and "spring plowing and summer weeding." In other words, this is the time for rest and relaxation after a year's toil, and for celebration as well.

The festivities reach their climax around the New Year's Eve and the New Year's Day, when there are continuous feasting and rejoicing amid the din of gong striking, drum beating and firecracker shooting. While the grown-ups occupy themselves with New Year dinner parties and mutual calls, the children enjoy the New Year entertainment such as fireworks and lantern splays, lion dance and other folk shows, visits to festival fairs, etc. Nothing is spared to make the celebrations joyous and memorable.

None of the other public festivals can compare with these two in grandeur. Women's Day (8 March), Youth Day (4 May), Children's Day (1 June) and the recently established Aged People's Day (9 of 9th lunar month) are festivals for particular sections of the population, although they are of course also the concern of all society. The Anniversary of the founding of the Communist Party of China (1 July) and Army Day (1 August) are both days of great significance, but they are more of commemoration days than of public festivals.

Of the many lesser traditional festivals, the Mid-Autumn Festival is perhaps the most popular. This holiday has 2,000 years of history in China. The 15th day of the 8th month of the lunar calendar marks the middle of autumn. The traditional food of the Mid-Autumn Festival is moon cakes. Give them as gifts or use them as bricks to build a house. The festival is a time for family members to gather together and enjoy the family harmony. And on the Mid-autumn night family members and friends gather to admire the full moon while eating their moon cakes under the beautiful moon.

Every ethnic and religious group in China has its own special festivals, as the Water-Sprinkling Festival of the Dai and Corban of the Muslims. These form an important part of the cultural and spiritual life of the groups concerned.

Many of these holidays had been observed for thousands of years until they mysteriously and suddenly fell out of practice during the Cultural Revolution. Despite the fatuous decline in the observance of traditional Chinese holidays, after all, 99 percent of the conversations you have with Chinese people are like the topic of traditional Chinese holidays.

Today, besides the summer and winter vacations, Chinese kids only get off from school for ten officially recognized national holidays every year, but there are many more folk holidays that are taken with varying degrees of seriousness throughout

China.

Notes

1. In large cities people throng the street, squares and parks in their holiday best.

   在大城市的街道上、广场中和公园里挤满了身着节日盛装的人们。

   in one's holiday(Sunday) best 指穿着节日盛装(最好的服装)。

2. In the evening these places are a blaze of light.

   夜晚,这些地方一片灯火辉煌。

   a blaze of light 指灯火通明;a blaze of color 指五彩缤纷。

3. the Gregorian solar calendar

   格里阳历,即目前通用的阳历。

   lunar calendar 指阴历,即农历。

4. Nothing is spared to make the celebrations joyous and memorable.

   不惜一切使得庆祝活动欢快而让人难以忘怀。

   spare no efforts(pains) 指不遗余力。

5. Aged People's Day (the Double Ninth Festival)

   每年阴历九月九日为"重阳节",又称"重九节";我国政府现将此日定为全国"敬老日"。

6. Of many lesser traditional festivals, the Mid-Autumn Festival is perhaps the most popular.

   在许多较次要的节日中,中秋节也许是最为大众所喜爱的节日。

   lesser 是 little 的比较级,只作定语,表示较小的、次要的或更少的。

7. the Water-Sprinkling Festival of the Dai

   泼水节,中国傣族和中南半岛某些民族的新年节日。根据我国傣族节期在傣历六七月间(清明前后十日左右)举行泼水节。节日期间,人们相互泼水祝福,并举行拜佛、赛龙舟等活动,为傣族一年中最盛大的传统节日。

Exercises:Mark the following statements with "T" or "F" according to TexB.

1. On National Day, main streets and public buildings are decorated with flags and flowers.

2. The celebrations of the Spring Festival take place in late January or early February and only last for a week.

3. Aged People's Day is on 9 of 9th lunar month, which is a public festival for the senior citizen.

4. Mid-Autumn Day is a time for family members to gather together and enjoy the family reunion.

5. Besides the summer and winter holidays, Chinese children have no other legal holidays.

Text C Holidays in the U.S.

There are so many American holidays, some of them are listed and explained, hope you might enjoy them.

1. Valentine's Day, February 14. This holiday is named for a Christian saint who was an example of love. Now, it is a holiday for lovers, husbands and wives, children, and anyone else who wants to remember this day. Parents and children often give cards or presents at this time. Men can give some chocolate or a few roses to their mother or girlfriend. Women can send a funny card to their boyfriend.

2. Easter, usually in early April. This is the most important Christian holiday, having a more religious tone than Christmas. For devout Christians, the days before Easter are solemn, because they remember the betrayal and crucifixion of Jesus. Easter itself is joyous because it commemorates the resurrection of Jesus, as well as spring. There are many pre-Christian symbols associated with Easter, such as eggs and flowers, symbolizing new life and fertility. Parents often hide colored eggs, or candy eggs, which children find during the Easter Egg Hunt and put in baskets. These eggs have supposedly been laid by the Easter Bunny. Traditionally, women often had a new dress or hat, an "Easter Bonnet", for this day. This is the best time of year to eat " jelly beans."

3. April Fool's Day, April 1. Don't be surprised if someone plays a trick on this day or tells you something that's not true.

4. Mother's Day, the second Sunday in May. On this day, you must send a card and a present to your mother.

5. Father's Day, the third Sunday in June. On this day, you must send a card and perhaps a present to your father.

6. Independence Day, July 4. This is the greatest patriotic holiday. On this day, you can eat watermelon, and at night you can usually find a fireworks display to attend. It's a good day to be invited to someone's house for an outdoor barbecue, or hear American traditional music on the radio.

7. Thanksgiving Day, the fourth Thursday in November. This holiday is celebrated by almost all Americans, and usually consists of a trip home for a huge meal

followed by hours and hours of televised football games. There are many typical foods for this day: turkey, bread stuffing, cranberries, squash, pumpkin pie. Some people go to a good restaurant to eat these foods. This day celebrates a meal between early settlers called Pilgrims and the Native Americans feel that this hospitality was betrayed, so they do not commemorate this event. It is a day for giving thanks for family and friends and for a plentiful harvest.

8. Christmas, December 25. The celebration often begins on Christmas Eve, December 24. On that day, you may enjoy attending a candlelight church service, for example a service of "Lessons and Carols", where you will hear the best known Christmas carols. That night, children hang up large stockings at the fireplace, where in the morning they find presents which their parents tell them have been left by Santa Claus. "Lavish" is a good word to describe this holiday, because houses are generally decorated with all kinds of ribbons, snowmen, perhaps a large tree with lights and hanging ornaments, candles, and other traditional figures. Most people spend a lot of money to buy presents for friends and family members.

There are many other holidays in the U.S., if you are interested in it, please read some books about them by yourself.

Notes

1. Valentine's Day 情人节,即圣瓦伦丁节
2. Christian saint 基督教圣人
3. Easter 复活节
4. the betrayal and crucifixion of Jesus 基督被背叛和钉上十字架
5. fertility 丰饶,富裕
6. the Easter Bunny 复活节的兔子
7. jelly beans 软心豆粒糖
8. patriotic 爱国的
9. barbecue 烧烤,常被称为 BBQ
10. Thanksgiving Day 感恩节
11. a trip home for a huge meal 回家吃一顿大餐
12. turkey, bread stuffing, cranberries, squash, pumpkin pie 火鸡、夹馅面包、越橘、西葫芦、南瓜馅饼
13. Pilgrims 指清教徒。1620 年,一批英国人在马萨诸塞州建立了普利茅斯殖民地。这些人常被称做 Pilgrims,即清教徒前辈移民。每年美国的感

恩节都要庆祝1621年那些清教徒前辈移民与马萨诸塞州沿海的北美土著居民共享的收获胜宴。

14. hospitality（对客人等的）殷勤招待
15. commemorate（借仪式、活动等）庆祝,纪念
16. Lessons and Carols 布道和颂歌
17. Santa Claus 圣诞老人（源自儿童的守护圣人圣尼古拉之名）
18. lavish 挥霍,浪费
19. ornament 装饰,摆设

Exercises: Answer the following questions according to Text C.

1. What is Valentine's Day? How do people spend it?
2. Which is the most important Christian holiday? Why? Is it a sad day?
3. On which day, people are free to play a trick with others?
4. When are Mother's Day and Father's Day? What will people do for their parents?
5. Why didn't the Native Americans celebrate Thanksgiving Day? What are the typical foods?
6. Why did children hang up large stockings at the fireplace?

Unit 4 Post Office

Study Structure
Text A (Intensive Reading): Postal and Telephone Services
Dialogues
New Words and Expressions
Exercises
Text B (Extensive Reading): How did Stamps Come into Use
Text C (Supplementary Reading): Modern Communication

Summary of the Text

  This unit is informative. You'll know postal and telephone services in Britain and U.S., how stamps came into use, and some modern communication in the age of information. In addition, you'll know what the I.D.D. phones mean. Therefore, when traveling, they help you to communicate with your family, friends, business partners easily and efficiently.

Text A Postal and Telephone Services

  In Britain, post offices normally open on weekdays from 8:30 or 9:00 am to 5:30 or 6:00 p.m. Pillar-boxes in streets are painted red.
  Postal service can be divided into two classes: first-class mail and second-class mail. The former has great priority but its rates are higher. The advantage is that the delivery is quicker. The latter is usually delivered 24 hours later than the former.
  If you like, you can send postcards. They can be sent by either service at letter rate. Do remember not to send parcels by letter post because it is very expensive. You can send your parcel by parcel post. It is slower but it is much cheaper.
  The U.S. postal system was derived from the colonial service established by England. Postage stamps were first used in 1847 (they had already been adopted in Britain in 1939). As the population moved west, during the 19th century, the long distances involved created the problem of speed delivery. At that time, the Pony Express provided fast mail service between different places. Expert riders, chosen

for their light weight, rode horses in relays. Each rider would ride from one "Home station" to another thus covering from 75 to 100 miles, and changing horses, from 6 to 8 times. After a rest period, he carried the mail in the other direction.

Nowadays, the U.S. Postal Services has competitors. Courier services send or transmit messages; parcels and freight are delivered by a number of companies. There are two ways of sending things safely through the post office: registered and certified mail. Certified letter is much cheaper. You can have mail sent to you through General Delivery in any town. It will be held ten days, or up to a month if the sender writes "Please hold 30 days" on the envelope. Using the zip code will speed up delivery.

Telephones provide a simple and efficient means to function from day to day. Several times in the course of a day, you may consult by phone with persons on travel - related matters. Your phone saves time and money. If you want to ask the time schedule, check the prices, take a train, bus or plane, you can call to find out schedules, prices and other information and to make a reservation. Phones are easily accessible. There are pay (or public) ones in which you deposit coins or cards to make a call. It is fairly convenient for your travel.

Generally speaking, it is very easy to find a public telephone. Public phones are located in bus and railroad stations, airports, stores, hotels, restaurants, gasoline stations, on numerous street corners and in most office buildings. However, remember, you cannot usually make telephone calls from post offices.

Dialogues

Dialogue A: At the Post Office

A: Good morning.
B: Good morning. I'd like to send some postcards and a letter to the Netherlands. Could you tell me the postage, please?
A: One dollar for each postcard. The postage for the letter depends on the weight and what kind of mail you'd like to use: ordinary, registered or special delivery?
B: I'd like to send this by registered airmail.

Dialogue B: Posting Registered Letter with A.R.

A: Anything I can do for you?
B: Yes. I'd like to have two letters to send to Canada. How much is the postage,

please?

A: How do you like to send them? Ordinary or registered?

B: I've not decided yet. I'd like to have your opinions.

A: What are the contents?

B: Some important business documents.

A: I suggest you send them by registered letter with A.R.

B: What do you mean by registered letter with A.R? What's the difference between registered letter and registered letter with A.R?

A: By registered letter with A.R, you'll get an acknowledgement of receipt(A.R.) after the letter has been delivered.

B: That's fine. Please get them sent by registered letter with A.R.

A: Oh, you've written the address in pencil. That won't do.

B: I'm sorry. Let me re-write it in ink. How about that letter?

A: That's quite right.

New Words and Expressions

1. normally /ˈnɔːməli/ adv. 通常,一般地
2. pillar /ˈpilə/ n. 柱状物
   pillar-box /ˈpiləˈbɔks/ 圆柱状的邮筒
3. divide /diˈvaid/ v. 把……分成……
4. priority /praiˈɔrəti/ n. 优先(权)
5. advantage /ədˈvɑːntidʒ/ n. 利益、优点、长处
6. parcel /ˈpɑːsl/ n. 包裹
7. derive /diˈraiv/ v. 起源
8. colonial /kəˈləunjəl/ adj. 殖民地的
9. establish /iˈstæbliʃ/ v. 建立,设立
10. adopt /əˈdɔpt/ v. 采用,采纳
11. involve /inˈvɔlv/ v. 卷入
12. competitor /kəmˈpetitə/ n. 竞争者
13. courier /ˈkuriə/ n. (递送重要文件的)信差
14. transmit /trænzˈmit/ v. 寄送
15. freight /freit/ n. 货物,(货物)运输
16. register /ˈredʒistə/ v. 挂号
17. certify /ˈsɔːtifai/ v. 保证
18. zip code /zip//kəud/ n. 邮政编码

19. efficient	/ɪˈfɪʃənt/	adj. 有效的
20. function	/ˈfʌŋkʃən/	n. 功能，作用
21. consult	/kənˈsʌlt/	v. 查询
22. schedule	/ˈʃedjuːl/	n. 日程表
23. reservation	/ˌrezəˈveɪʃn/	n. 订购，预约
24. downtown	/ˈdaʊnˈtaʊn/	n. 市中心
25. accessible	/əkˈsesəbl/	adj. 容易获得的
26. deposit	/dɪˈpɒzɪt/	v. 放置
27. locate	/ləʊˈkeɪt/	v. 位于，确定……的位置
28. ordinary	/ˈɔːdənrɪ/	adj. 普通的
29. registered	/ˈredʒɪstəd/	adj. 挂号的
30. opinion	/əˈpɪnjən/	n. 观点
31. content	/ˈkɒntent/	n. 内容
32. document	/ˈdɒkjumənt/	n. 文件
33. acknowledgement	/əkˈnɒlɪdʒmənt/	n. 承认
34. receipt	/rɪˈsiːt/	n. 收据

Notes

1. be derived from 起源于……，相当于 come from，也可使用 derive from，意义相同。
2. the Pony Express 骑马快速投递，是最初开始于美国蒙大拿州的圣·约瑟夫和加利福尼亚州的沙克拉门托两城之间的快速邮政服务。
3. in relays 轮番地，这里指各驿站之间的换马接力传递。
4. home station 指初始驿站。
5. in the other direction 指往回来的方向。
6. send or transmit messages 指收发信函。
7. zip code 邮政编码，zip 是 zone improvement program (plan) 的缩写，英国之称 postcode。
8. deposit coins or cards 投币或插卡。
9. Netherlands 指荷兰，面临北海的西欧国家，亦称为 Holland。
10. ordinary, registered or special delivery 普通信件，挂号信，特快专递。
11. have one's opinion 征询某人的意见，常用短语 in one's opinion 根据某人的意见。
12. an acknowledgement of 承认。
13. in pencil 指用铅笔；in ink 指用钢笔。in 表示使用某种手段、方法、材料。

如 in English, in cash。

14. rewrite 表示重写，re-为前缀，表示重新做某事。

Useful Expressions and Patterns

1. What's the air mail rate to Europe?
   寄欧洲的航空邮资是多少?
2. Will you please weigh this parcel for me?
   请称一下这包裹好吗?
3. It is overweight, you have to pay extra.
   它超重了,您要另付超重费。
4. Do you think I should have it registered?
   你看我该把它挂号吗?
5. Tell me how to post a letter abroad, please.
   请告诉我怎样寄信到国外。
6. Please fill in the order form.
   请您填汇款单。
7. Please stick the stamps on upper right corner of the letter.
   请把邮票贴在信的右上角。
8. Please write down the postcode.
   请写上邮政编码。
9. By surface mail?
   普通邮递吗?
10. Please sign it under signature.
    请在签名栏下签名。

Exercises

Ⅰ. Answer the following questions according to Text A.

1. How many classes can postal services be divided into in Britain? What are they?
2. Why must you remember not to send parcels by letter post?
3. Where did the U.S. postal system come from?
4. In old days, what provided fast mail service between different places?
5. What are the safe ways of sending things through the post office?
6. Where are public phones located?

Ⅱ. Mark the following statements with "T"(True) or "F" (False) according to Test A.

1. In Britain, pillar-boxes in streets are painted green.
2. Post cards can only be mailed by first-class mail at letter rate.
3. During the 19th century, because people moved west, the problem of speed delivery appeared.
4. Certified letter is no cheaper than registered one.
5. It is very easy to find a public telephone at the Post Office.

Ⅲ. Translation.

1. Translate the following sentences into Chinese.
1) In most cases, the address follows the order of house number first, then street, town, state, postal code and finally the country name.
2) Traditionally, the complimentary close is placed two spaces below the body of the letter, to the right of the page, in line with the date block at the top.
3) Every well-constructed business letter is made up of ten essential parts, namely the heading, the inside address, the salutation, the subject heading, the body of the letter, the complimentary close, the senders signature and identification, the designation, etc.
4) There are two ways of sending things safely through the post office: registered and certified mail.
5) Several times in the course of a day, you may consult by phone with persons on travel-related matters.

2. Translate the following into English.
1)目前,我们仍然大量使用信件进行业务交往,因为它安全可靠,且费用低。
2)电子信件使个人和公司能够在全球范围内十分方便有效地,而且又非常经济可靠地进行交流。
3)处在信息时代的人们充分利用电报、传真和电子邮件来传递最新信息。
4)据预测,在今后的几年里,各种通讯方式将在各行各业中得到更迅速、更广泛的发展。
5)在商务信件中不可把与业务无关的事写在信中,以免造成误会。
6)在不同的国家里,书写信头时日期的表达法也不尽相同,千万别混淆。

Ⅳ. Complete the following dialogue.

C = Clerk   G = Guest

C: Good morning! Can I help you?
G: I'd like to _____(把这个包裹寄给在美国的母亲)。

How can I do it?

C: _____(您要怎样邮寄,空运还是海运)?

G: How long does it take by surface?

C: _____(大约两到三个月).

G: That's too long. This is a Christmas gift I'm sending. _____(我想让它寄到美国)before the Christmas mail rush.

C: In that case, I would recommend sending it by air.

G: _____ (空寄有多快)?

C: It will be there in 10 to 15 days.

G: That's much faster. _____(那么,就空寄吧)?

C: Very good. _____(请填写这张表)?

G: Yes, of course. . . . Here is the form.

C: Thank you. _____(请把包打开检查一下)?

G: Sure.

C: Thank you. You can put it back in now. (She weighs the parcel) It's 1 kilogram. It's 81.50 yuan.

G: _____ (给你100元).

C: Thank you. And here is your 18.50 yuan _____(找零和收据).

Ⅴ. **Vocabulary and Structure.**

1. Fill in the blank with the words or expressions given below. Change the form where necessary.

be located in, be divided into, give priority to, derive from, generally speaking, adopt, up to, speed up, find out, make a reservation.

1) _____ , the weather has been mild this winter.

2) We _____ two children whose parents were killed in an accident.

3) The new office building _____ a suburb.

4) A large house _____ flats.

5) He _____ great pleasure _____ traveling abroad.

6) The government _____ reforming the legal system.

7) I just _____ that the payment is due tomorrow.

8) He _____ for three nights at the hotel.

9) _____ now, he's done a lot of work.

10) The boss told his men to _____ their work.

2. Match the following two columns.

A 避暑胜地　　　　　　　a. Tourism and Vacation Zones
B 优惠政策　　　　　　　b. annual receipts
C 高消费旅行者　　　　　c. preferential policies
D 金融交易　　　　　　　d. handicrafts and tourist souvenirs
E 信息途径快捷　　　　　e. Summer resort
F 年收入　　　　　　　　f. International Travel Act
G 自然及文化型生态旅游　g. financial transactions
H 手工艺品及旅游纪念品　h. quick access to information
I 旅游度假区　　　　　　i. nature-and-culture-based ecotourism
J 国际旅游法　　　　　　j. high-spend visitors

3. Multiple Choices

1) It was in 1950 that the first package holiday built around _____ was organized.
   A. air transport　　　　　B. water transport
   C. Grand tourism　　　　 D train transport

2) Tourists take vacations not to _____.
   A. relax and have a good time
   B. learn another culture.
   C. satisfy various needs and wants.
   D. make profit.

3) _____ is not psychological needs.
   A. Security　　　　　　　B. Activity
   C. Affection　　　　　　　D. Self-esteem

4) _____ can be considered the end or goal of leisure.
   A. Self - actualization　　B. Esteem
   C. Aesthetics　　　　　　D. To know and understand

5) Tourists seeking rest and relaxation generally require _____.
   A. good food　　　　　　B. good but cheap accommodation
   C. good transportation　　D. nearest resort

Ⅵ. Situational dialogue: Make up a dialogue according to the given situation.

This is a dialogue between a postal clerk and a girl named Kitty. Kitty wants to send some postcards and a letter to England. She doesn't know the postage, time to mail. So she asked the clerk.

Ⅶ. Mini Dialogues.

1. A: What's the postage on these letters to Hong Kong, please?

   B: It's ﹩1 by surface mail and ﹩2 by air mail. So it comes to 6 dollars altogether.

   A: Thank you.

   B: You are welcome.

2. A: Can I help you, Miss?

   B: I want to send this letter to Paris.

   A: Airmail?

   B: Yes. It doesn't take very long, does it?

   A: About 6 days ... Good, the letter is just about the right weight. Anything else, Miss?

   B: No, thanks. How much is it?

Ⅷ. Practical Writing.

Letter of Application (求职信)

25 Thimbler Road, Canley
Coventry, CV4 8FN
Tel: 213-2417785
8, Sept. 1998

Dear Sir or Madam,

  I'm writing in reply to your advertisement in Printers' Post for an assistant to the Print Production Manager.

  I am 33 years old, married with two sons. I am at present the Paper Buyer for the Offset Company; I have been in this position for three years. Before I was promoted I worked for six years in various departments including the finishing department, and I have some experience of the color processes. I had contacts with colleagues in other departments.

  I have been able to find sources of supply which have brought down our costs by 4.5%.

  As you will see from this letter, my English is good; I have passed Certificate Examination.

  I hope I may be of interest to you, and I look forward to hearing from you.

Yours faithfully,
Ann Jones

First Certificate Examination(剑桥一级证书考试)

Structure analysis

There are three important points which should be included in a letter of application. In the following table, you are given some useful patterns and expressions under each of three points. You can add more of them.

Refer to advertisement.

1. With reference to your advertisement in the Printer's Post.
2. I would like to apply for the post of Personal Assistant.
3. I've seen your advertisement in the newspaper and I am interested in applying for the post of Secretary to the Sales Manager.
4. I'm interested in you advertisement for an Export Sales Manager.
5. I should like to apply for the position of Sales Representative as advertised in yesterday's...

Describing your experiences.

1. As you can see from the enclosed curriculum vitae, I have had long experience in difficult fields.
2. In my last job the administrative side was extremely important and I learnt to work under pressure.
3. In my last job there was a lot of work using computers.
4. In my present job, public relation is very important aspect I run the office independently.

Reasons to choose the new job.

1. However, although I like my present job, I would now prefer a post offering more responsibility/chances of promotion.
2. I'm happy in my present job. However, I am now looking for a post where I can use my knowledge of languages.
3. I now feel should like the greater challenge of managing a group of hotels.
4. I'm delighted to have the possibility of employment with a company where I can use my financial knowledge.

Simulated writing.

1. Read the letter of application again and try to fill in the following Application Form with information from the letter.

THE PRINTER GROUP
APPLICATION FOR EMPLOYMENT CONFIDENTIAL
IN BLOCK LETTERS

Position applied for 1. _____

Full name 2._____
Address 3._____
_____
Tel 4._____
Exams/diplomas obtained 5._____
Work experiences 6._____
_____
Date 7._____
Signature 8._____
structure analysis

Text B How did Stamps Come into Use

When you send a letter or a postcard, you have to put stamps on the envelope or in the card. When did people first begin to use stamps? Who was the first to think of this idea?

In the early 19th century, people did not use stamps. They had to pay postage when they received letters. They were unhappy about this, especially when they paid for a letter that they did not wish to receive at all. The postage rate was high at that time, because the post offices had to send many people to collect the postage.

Rowland Hill, a schoolmaster in England, was the first to put forward a proposal to use stamps and put them on envelopes before they sent the letters. The post office could simply put seals on the stamps. In this way, the post office did not need to send postmen to collect postage. It only needed to send fewer postmen to deliver letters. That was a good idea and the government finally accepted it.

On May 6, 1840, post offices throughout England began to sell stamps-" One Penny" black stamps and " Two Pence" blue stamps.

Notes

1. the postage rate 指邮资。
2. collect the postage 指收邮资。
3. Rowland Hill 罗兰·黑尔，英国的一位校长，他首先提出在信封上贴邮票的建议。
4. put forward a proposal 提出建议。
   put sth. forward = propose or suggest sth. for discussion. 如, put forward an argument, a plan, etc.

5. cover postage 代替邮资。
6. put seals on the stamps. 在邮票上盖章。
7. " One Penny " black stamps. 一便士的黑色邮票。
8. " Two Pence " blue stamps. 两便士的蓝色邮票。

Exercises: Mark the following statements with "T" (True) or "F" (False) according to Text B.

1. People didn't use stamps until the early 19th century.
2. In the early 19th century, people had to pay postage when they received letters.
3. The postage rate was high at that time, because the letters are difficult to send.
4. Using stamps is a good idea and the government adopted in the end.
5. At the beginning, there are two kinds of stamps: one is black and the other is green.

Text C Modern Communication

We live in an age of information. It is predicted that information will be the most important commodity in many industries; therefore, telephone communication plays an increasingly important role in our life. Technological advances have given us satellites, wide - area telephone services, mobile telephones, automatic telephone - answering services, telegraphs, telexes, faxes and E- mail, and so on. They are very useful and helpful modern communications.

Telephones are the most popular part of modern communication because they provide instant and efficient communication and they are not very expensive. People use telephones to discuss business, give invitations, ask favors, convey other useful messages or simply have a chat. There are basically four - types of phone calls : Local calls, long distance calls, intercom or conference calls and assistance calls. A station - to - station long distance call is much less expensive than a person - to - person call, while the latter offers more privacy. With the I.D.D phones available, both terms are seldom used nowadays. A collect call means the person who receives the call pays. This kind of call is more expensive, but it is convenient for the caller if he does not have money with him.

Telegrams are still used to relay information where telephones are not popularized. Telex, Fax and E - mail are mostly used in various businesses.

The electronic mail application lets us send message to people in the next office, in America, or anywhere in the " data communication world ". Most companies are moving in the direction of linking their computers, including PCs, together in a computer network. This enables employees to route messages to each other via E-mail. A message can be a note, letter, report, chart, or even a procedures manual. Each employee at a company is assigned an "electronic mailbox" on disk storage in which messages are received and stored. An employee "opens" and "reads" his or her electronic mail by simply going to the nearest workstation and recalling messages from storage.

Electronic mail is becoming a very common business use of computers. And also, we can have a visual communication by equipping a PC-camera in a computer. The future stretched before modern communication will be in beams of crystal sunlight.

Notes

1. it is predicted 据预测，类似的短语有 it is said, it is reported 等。
2. commodity 名词，商品。
3. play a role in = play a part in 在……中起作用。
4. instant and efficient 及时有效的。
5. local calls, long distance calls, intercom or conference calls and assistance calls 本地电话、长途电话、内部或会议电话、辅助电话。
6. a station-to-station long distance call 叫号电话，打电话的人同意跟任何接电话的人讲话。
   a person-to-person call 叫人电话，打电话的人只跟指定的人讲话。
7. the I.D.D phones - the International Direct Dialing phones 国际直播电话。
8. telex - telegraph exchange, teleprinter exchange or teletypewriter exchange 电传系统，使用电传打印机的传送系统。
9. fax - Facsimile telegraph 传真。
10. E-mail - electronic mail 电子邮件。
11. a PC-camera 即 Computer Vision telephone 电脑可视电话。

Exercises: Answer the following questions according to Text C.

1. Why does telephone communication play an increasingly role in our life?
2. How many modern communications can we use? Please list them.
3. What's the reason that telephones are the most popular part of modern communication?
4. What are basically four-types of phone calls?
5. How can we use E-mail?
6. What about the future of modern communication?

Unit 5 Hotel Services

Study structure

Text A (Intensive Reading): Hotel Services
Dialogues
New Words and Expressions
Exercises
Text B (Extensive Reading): Housekeeping Development
Text C (Supplementary Reading): The Small Country Inn

Summary of the Text

Various types of hotels and functions of different hotel organizations have been introduced in this unit. Housekeeping department as the main component must take the responsibility of offering clean environment and making guests as comfortable as possible. In addition, the small country inn has all its advantages. Do you want to know about its characteristics and origin?

Text A Hotel Services

The major trend in hotel services today is toward the high-speed and convenience. Guests expect to find almost everything they need right in the hotel. To meet the requirements of guests, a hotel will leave no means untried. There are different levels and kinds of hotels. At the top are the luxury or deluxe hotels. At the bottom are those that provide merely a place to sleep. For the various purposes, there are commercial or transient hotels, motel hotels, resort hotels, residential hotels and convention hotels. Different services are offered in different levels and types of hotels.

Generally speaking, regular hotel services include the front office services, chamber services, restaurant services, recreation services, shop services and security services.

The front office deals with such questions as room reservations, guest reception and information response to guests' inquiry. A reservationist's job is to take reservations, cancellations and revisions, and write and send out the hotel's letters of conformation. Since the communications are well developed, advance reservations can be made by telephone, telegraph or telex. Then the hotel can confirm a guest's booking immediately with a reply telex and the incoming telex from the guest, which can be kept as the confirmation of the guest's booking. Guests are received at the front desk of the hotel where they register, pick up their keys and mail, request information, deposit their valuables and pay their bills. It is called the reception area where the reception services are given. The front desk employees work as the representatives of the hotel and plays an important role in the business success.

Chamber services refers to what chambermaids need to do with the hotel rooms in which guests stay. For example, tidy up rooms, make the beds, hand out the things supplied by the housekeeping department, collect and deliver clothing for the laundry and so on.

A restaurant is an indispensable part of a hotel. Food and beverage are provided, which account for two fifths to half of a hotel's profit. In large hotels, the restaurant is made up of grill room, different bars, cafeteria and room service. The food and beverage department employees, especially waiters, waitresses and bartenders, play an extremely important role in contribution to the success of services. A good waiter should serve the customers with a cordial smile, plenty of courtesy, sincere effort and efficiency.

Recreation services are for guest's pleasure and relaxation. Many hotels contain recreational facilities such as ballrooms, auditoriums, swimming pools or health clubs. There are modern stereo and lighting equipments for guests to sing and dance to the music. Guests can also get some physical exercises by making use of sport equipments.

Most hotels have a shop where you can buy some necessities of life, travel items, handicrafts, special local products, food and drinks, snacks and so on. Customers feel pleasant to get such service because they don't have to walk a long way for the things they need.

Few hotels felt the need to offer security services until recent years. In many large hotels (particularly in downtown areas), a security department is now essential. Security personnel work not only to protect hotel guests and their belongings, but also to protect hotel property.

Different categories of hotels serve different clientele. The commercial hotel provides services essentially for transients, many of whom travel on business. Many city hotels and diversely located motels fall into this group. The services offered by commercial hotels and motels are very similar to those of hotels. But the one distinguishing aspect of motels is free parking on the premises. Few hotels can offer this feature to all guests.

Resort hotels are located in vacation areas or scenic spots, which cater for vacationers and recreation-minded people with the help of natural enviroment.

Convention hotels aim their services largely at the convention trade. Such hotels all feature a wide variety of restaurants, banquet rooms, meeting rooms and convention / exhibition halls. Some can accommodate up to 4,000 guests at a single convention.

Residential hotels cater for people who do not wish to keep houses themselves and rent accommodations on a seasonal basis or even permanently. A residential hotel is usually an apartment building offering maid service, a dining room meal service and possibly a cocktail lounge. The food and beverage department is only a small part which brings convenience to residents.

With the development of hotel industry, there will be more complex departments offering additional services. The reputation of a hotel is decided by the degrees of comfort and service given to the guest. The motto—"Reputation first, customer foremost" will never changed.

Dialogues

Dialogue A: Checking-in at the hotel

A: May I help you, Sir?
B: Yes, I'd like to check in. My name is Bill Smith. Miss Wang from Youth Travel Agency has booked a single room for me.
A: Let me check. Oh, yes, you have a reservation for a single room on the fifth floor.
B: Does it have a bath?
A: Yes, certainly.
B: Is there a telephone in the room?
A: Yes, all of our rooms have phones.
B: Then do you provide meals?
A: Oh, yes, we've a very good restaurant. We serve breakfast from Six to nine, lunch from eleven to one and dinner from five to ten.
B: Ok, I'd like to have this room for a week.

A: Would you please fill in this registration card?

B: Yes.

A: Here is the key to Room 512. I'll find a porter to take your luggage up.

B: Thanks a lot.

A: You are welcome. If there's anything you need, just call the reception.

B. Ok, thank you.

Dialogue B

G = Guest   A = Floor Attendant

G: Good evening. This is Mr Green in Room 518.

A: Good evening, Mr. Smith. What can I do for you?

G: I'm going to attend a seminar at 7:30 tomorrow morning. I'm afraid I can't get up early enough. I'd like to request an early morning call.

A: Ok, Mr. Green. When would you like us to call you?

G: Well, I am not sure how long it should take to get to Jingjiang Hotel. Is it easy to take a taxi here?

A: Yes, of course. Taxis are infallibly available in front of the entrance at any time. It usually takes about 20 minutes to get to that hotel.

G: In that case, please wake me up at 5:30. Then I can have the time to wash and eat my breakfast.

A: 5:30? Ok. So we'll call you at 5:30. All right. Good night, Mr. Green.

G: Thank you. Good night.

New Words and Expressions

1. major   /meidʒə/   adj. 主要的
2. trend   /trend/   n. 趋势
3. convenience   /kən'vi:niəns/   n. 方便
4. level   /levl/   n. 水平
5. luxury   /'lʌkʃəri/   n. 奢侈,奢侈品
6. deluxe   /di'lʌks/   adj. 豪华的,奢华的
7. commercial   /kə'mə:ʃl/   adj. 商业的
8. transient   /'trænziənt/   adj. 短暂的,路过的
9. resort   /ri'zɔ:t/   n. 胜地,度假之地
10. residential   /ˌrezi'denʃl/   adj. 居住的
11. offer   /'ɔfə/   vt. 提供
12. type   /taip/   n. 类型

13.	recreation	/ˌrekriˈeiʃnl/	n. 文艺,娱乐
14.	security	/siˈkjuəriti/	n. 安全
15.	reservation	/ˌrezəˈveiʃən/	n. 预定
16.	reception	/riˈsepʃən/	n. 接待,接受
17.	response	/risˈpɔns/	n. 回应,反应
18.	reservationist	/ˌrezəˈveiʃənist/	n. 预定员
19.	cancellation	/ˌkænsəˈleiʃən/	n. 取消,撤消
20.	revision	/riˈviʒən/	n. 修正,校订
21.	confirmation	/ˌkɔnfəˈmeiʃən/	n. 确定,核实
22.	telegraph	/ˈteligrɑːf/	n. 电报
23.	telex	/ˈteleks/	n. 用户电报
24.	reply	/riˈplai/	vt. 回复,答复
25.	register	/ˈredʒistə/	vt. 登记
26.	deposit	/diˈpɔzit/	vt. 存放
27.	valuable	/ˈvæljuəbl/	n. 贵重物品
28.	employee	/ˌemplɔiˈiː/	n. 雇员
29.	representative	/ˌrepriˈzentətiv/	n. 代理,代表
30.	chamber	/ˈtʃeimbə/	n. 房间,寝室
31.	chambermaid	/ˈtʃeimbəˈmeid/	n. 女服务员
32.	indispensable	/ˌindisˈpensəbl/	adj. 必不可少的
33.	beverage	/ˈbevəridʒ/	n. 饮料
34.	profit	/ˈprɔfit/	n. 利润
35.	grill	/gril/	n. 烤架,烧烤
36.	cafeteria	/ˌkæfiˈtiəriə/	n. 自助食堂
37.	bartender	/ˈbɑːtendə/	n. 酒吧间招待员
38.	cordial	/ˈkɔːdjəl/	adj. 热诚的,亲切的
39.	courtesy	/ˈkəːtəsi/	n. 礼貌,殷勤
40.	necessity	/niˈsesiti/	n. 必需品
41.	handicraft	/ˈhædiˈkrɑːft/	n. 工艺品
42.	auditorium	/ˌɔːdiˈtɔːriəm/	n. 礼堂
43.	stereo	/ˈstiəriəu/	n. 立体声
44.	clientele	/ˌkliːɔnˈtel/	n. 委托人,顾客
45.	diversely	/daiˈvəːsli/	adv. 多样地,多变化地
46.	cater	/ˈkeitə/	vi. 迎合,投合
47.	accommodate	/əˈkɔmədeit/	vt. 容纳,供应

48. accommodation /əˈkɔmədeiʃən/   n. 膳宿供应
49. permanently /ˈpəːmənəntli/   adv. 永久地
50. lounge /laundʒ/   n. 休息处,休息室
51. motto /mɔtəu/   n. 格言,箴言
52. reputation /ˌrepjuˈteiʃən/   n. 名誉,声望
53. seminar /ˈseminaː/   n. 研讨会
54. infallibly /inˈfæləbli/   adv. 没有错误地,确实可靠地
55. feature /ˈfiːtʃə/   vt. 以……为特色
56. foremost /ˈfɔːməust/   adj. 最重要的,最先的

Notes

1. meet the requirements 满足需要。
2. leave no means untried 没有哪种办法没尝试过。(意指:想尽各种办法。) "untried"是过去分词作宾语补足语,如:We leave nothing undone.
3. deal with 处理,应付。
4. do with 对付,处置。
   如:How do you do with the untamed elephant?(你如何对付那头野象的?)
5. hand out 分发。
6. account for 意思是占……。
   如:Girl students account for 70% of the class.(女生占这班人数的70%)
7. health club 健身中心,健身俱乐部。
8. fall into 属于。
   如:This falls into the same category.(这属于同一范畴。)
9. on the premises 在……前提下;在建筑物内。
10. aim at 目的在于……
11. cater for 投合,迎合。
    如:This health club caters for those who wants to keep fit.(这个健身俱乐部迎合那些想要保持身体健康的人的需要。)
12. check in 登记入宿。
13. Travel Agency 旅行社。
14. have a reservation for 预定。
15. fill in the registration card 填写登记卡。
16. Reputation first, customer foremost 信誉第一,顾客至上。

Useful Expressions and Patterns

1. 预定和付账时用语

1) Do you have a reservation? Or Have you made a reservation?
   您预定了吗?
2) May we have a double room for those dates?
   那个日期内,我们可以有一套双人间吗?
3) Is breakfast included?
   包括早餐吗?
4) My wife is a light sleeper. We'd like a quiet room if possible.
   我妻子睡眠很轻,如果可能的话,我们想要一套安静的房间。
5) A friend of mine recommended your hotel to me.
   我的一位朋友向我推荐贵宾馆。
6) Oh, sorry, the rooms are all booked up. Would you like me to get in touch with somewhere else for you?
   哦,对不起,客房全满了,您是否愿意让我为您联系一下其他地方?
7) How would you like to pay, in cash or by credit card?
   您想如何付款,用现金还是信用卡?
8) How do you cover your expenses?
   您如何付账?
9) Sorry, we don't accept personal check.
   抱歉,我们不收私人支票。
10) What kind of check have you got?
    您用什么支票?

2. 对房间不满时用语

1) I'm not at all happy with my room.
   我对我的房间一点也不满意。
2) I'm simply shocked to find the room of an expensive hotel in such an intolerable condition.
   看到一个收费昂贵的饭店的客房脏乱到让人无法忍受,我简直非常惊讶。

Exercises

I. Answer the following questions according to text A.

1. What are the two main important aspects in hotel services?
2. How many types of hotels are mentioned in the text?
3. What questions does the front office deal with?
4. Whom do you contact with if you want to have your clothes washed?
5. Why is a restaurant indispensable part of a hotel?
6. How are recreation services offered to guests?
7. How can we distinguish motels from other hotels?
8. Where are resort hotels located?

II. Mark the following statements with "T" (True) or "F" (False) according to Text A.

1. Reservations belong to the task of housekeeping department.
2. The front desk workers are in the important position.
3. Since waiters or waitresses aren't allowed to accept tips, they don't have to give better services to customers.
4. You can't join in any recreational activities because it'll cost you more money to stay in the hotel.
5. Motels are in the category of commercial hotels.
6. Some families can buy the suites of the residential hotels as their home.

III. Translation.

1. Translate the following sentences into Chinese.
1) Since being away from home is necessary component of tourism, its development as a mass industry depend on modern means of rapid and inexpensive transportation.
2) The tourist industry is not a single entity. It consists of Many different kinds of enterprises that offer different services to the traveler, such as transportation, accommodations, catering, tour operators, travel agents and so on.
3) It is possible to distinguish between two general types of tours. One is the holiday package that has a resort hotel as its destination. The second is the guided tour that features sightseeing or some other special attraction.
4) The employee who checks in arriving guests and assigns them to there is the room clerk.

5) When the guest arrives, the room clerk checks its reservation or the availability of rooms if the guest does not have a confirmed reservation.

2. Translate the following into English.
1) 旅馆主要分为四大类:商务旅馆、旅游旅馆、汽车旅馆和居住旅馆。
2) 豪华型宾馆尽可能地为旅客提供最舒适的环境和方便的设施。
3) 餐饮部在宾馆管理中起着非常重要的作用。
4) 为了节省开支,有些宾馆在淡季歇业,到旺季来临时再开业。
5) 事实上,汽车旅馆提供的服务与其他旅馆所提供的服务几乎是一样的。
6) 一个宾馆主要由前台、客房、餐饮、商务等几大部门组成。

IV. Complete the following dialogue.

A. Good evening. Swan Hotel. Can I help you?

B. Good evening. I'm _____ to Harbin next weekend and a friend _____ your hotel to me.

A. Next weekend, you say? Well, we do still have one or two vacancies. How many nights _____?

B. Oh! Just Two.

A. Two nights... And when _____ ... Friday or Saturday?

B. Friday.

A. Do you need _____?

B. A single, please.

A. Let me just check for you. (Pause) Yes, I can _____ for those night. You are lucky because singles are hard to find at this time of year.

B. I see. And _____ the price, please?

A. _____ per night, including breakfast.

B. So, can I _____ now, please?

A. Certainly. _____, please?

B. Li Fang.

A. Yes, thank you, Miss Li. I've _____ then. And we'll look forward to seeing you next Friday.

B. Thank you so much.

A. _____. Byebye.

B. Goodbye!

V. Vocabulary and Structure.

1. Fill in the blank with the words or expressions given below. Change the form where necessary.

> Confirmation; reserve; cashier; illustrate; describe; develop the habit of; on the premises; direct...to; for pleasure; be similar to

1) The policemen think that the thief is still _____.
2) —Are you here on business?
   —No, I am here _____. It is my holiday this week.
3) Many Americans early _____ living permanently in hotels.
4) This paper is a _____ form that shows a reservation record.
5) Operator, connect me with the _____, please? I want to check out.
6) We've _____ two adjacent rooms with twin beds.
7) We should _____ our energies to the management of our hotel.
8) A typical travel agency has a rack of colourful brochures that _____ the delights offered by a wide variety of tours.
9) Retail travel services _____ clothing stores, expect that they sell intangible services rather than tangible goods.
10) Here are the brochures that _____ the tours.

2. Match the following two columns.

   A. 外汇收入　　　　　　a. tourist operator
   B. 出境旅游　　　　　　b. tourism bureau
   C. 包价旅游　　　　　　c. the foreign exchange receipts
   D. 包机航班　　　　　　d. out bound tourism
   E. 旅游经营商　　　　　e. the International Civil Aviation Organization
   F. 边境手续　　　　　　f. en route
   G. 国际民航组织　　　　g. Charter flights
   H. 旅游局　　　　　　　h. net earnings
   I. 在途中　　　　　　　i. Package tours
   J. 净收入　　　　　　　j. frontier formalities

3. Multiple Choices.

1) The golden age of the Grand Tour was the _____ century, particularly the 30 years before the outbreak of the French Revolution.
   A. 17th　　　　　　　　B. 18th
   C. 19th　　　　　　　　D. 16th

2) Some hotels in the United States can _____ more than three thousand people.
   A. commode　　　　　　B. accommodate

    C. bring in   D. contain

3) What kind of tourism is internal tourism plus outbound tourism.
    A. International tourism   B. Internal tourism
    C. Domestic tourism   D. National tourism

4) The World Tourism Organization, which is located in _____, is the only organization that represents all national and official tourism interests.
    A. Paris   B. Madrid
    C. Hawaii   D. Belgium

5) The operators of package tour usually _____ the public's need as fully as possible.
    A. cater for   B. serve
    C. make up   D. clear up

6) The chapter _____ five parts.
    A. divide   B. falls into
    C. separate   D. classify

7) _____ has led to growing demand for tourism both at home and abroad, and the expansion and improvement in associated facilities.
    A. Increased leisure time and improved incomes
    B. Low cost
    C. The economic recession
    D. A lot of holidays

8) Tourists take vocations not to _____.
    A. relax and have a good time
    B. learn another culture
    C. satisfy various needs and wants
    D. make profit

9) Tourists seeking rest and relaxation generally require _____.
    A. good food
    B. good but cheap accommodation
    C. good transportation
    D. nearest resort

10) Imports from the U.S.A _____ 50% of the total.
    A. occupy   B. hold
    C. capture   D. account for

VI. Situational dialogue.

Make up a dialogue according to the given situation.

This is the dialogue between Doorman and Guest. A taxi stops in front of Cherry Hotel. A doorman steps forward to open the door for the guest. The doorman greets the guest first. Then he helps to take out the baggage for the guest and tells the guest where he can check in.

VII. Mini Dialogues.

Dialogues A

Scene: A guest walks to the Reception Desk.

R = Receptionist   G = Guest

R: Good evening, Sir. Can I help you?

G: Yes, please. May I have a room in your hotel?

R: Have you made reservation?

G: I'm afraid not.

R: It is peak season now. All the rooms are booked up.

G: Oh, bad luck. Are there any other hotels nearby?

R: Yes, there are. Would you like me to get in touch with one?

G: Yes, do please.

R: There are rooms available in Swan Hotel. It's just five minutes' walk along this road.

G: Thank you very much.

R: You are welcome. (I'm always at your service.)

Dialogues B: Showing the guest to his room.

A: Your room is on the fifth floor. We may as well go up by the lift there and you'll be able to see some of the public rooms on the way.

B: That's a good idea. There is the dinning room, I see.

A: Yes, that's the dinning room for western food. There's another where you can eat Chinese food. And the café is on the fifth floor.

B: I suppose the hotel has a shop where I can get some odds and ends(零星日用品).

A: Yes, there's one just at the end of this corridor where you can buy souvenirs, stationary, sweets and so on. The barber shop and post office counter is round the corner, on the right...Here are the lifts. Shall we go up?

VIII. Practical Writing: Read the forms about laundry list and try to fill in the form.

DRY CLEANING

Room No. _____ Date _____

Print Name _____ Signature _____

Same day service: Order before 10:00, Delivered by 19:00

4 hours service (50% extra charge): Order between 08:00 and 16:00

Pressing only: Charge 60% of regular dry cleaning prices.

NOTICE:

1. Please fill in the blank with full name, room number and quantity of each article. Unless quantity is specified, our dry cleaning count must be accepted as correct.
2. We can not be responsible for shrinkage or fastness of color, unless necessary precautions are in advance.
3. Any claim for damage must be made within 24 hours, accompanied by the original list. The hotel will be responsible for loss or damage only up to 10 times the amount for dry cleaning.

GUEST COUNT 客人计数	HOTEL COUNT 饭店计数	GENTLEMEN 男装	PRICES F.E.C	CHARGES 收费
		Coat or Jacket 短装外套	12.00	
		Tie 领带	4.00	
		Overcoat 大衣	15.00	
		Raincoat 雨衣	15.00	
		Shirt 恤衫	7.00	
		Shorts 短裤	6.00	
		Suits(2pce) 西装一套	17.00	
		Sweater 毛衣	8.00	
		Trousers 西裤	8.00	
		Vest/Waistcoat 背心	5.00	
		LADIES		
		Blouse 恤衫		
		Sweater 毛衣	8.00	

第 5 单元 酒店服务

GUEST COUNT 客人计数	HOTEL COUNT 饭店计数	GENTLEMEN 男装	PRICES F.E.C	CHARGES 收费
		Coat or Jacket 外衣	10.00	
		Dress(plain) 连衣裙(简单)	12.00	
		Evening Dress 晚礼服	17.00	
		Overcoat 大衣	15.00	
		Raincoat 雨衣	15.00	
		Scarf 围巾	4.00	
		Shorts 短裤	6.00	
		Skirt 短裙	8.00	
		Skirt(pleated) 褶裙	17.00	
		Slacks 长裤	8.00	
		Suits(2 pce) 西装一套(两件)	17.00	
		BASIC CHARGE 基本费		
TOTAL NO. OF PIECES 总件数		EXPRESS SERVICE CHARGE 快洗服务费		
		10% SERVICE CHARGE:附加费		
SPECIAL INSTRUCTION 特别说明		总计 GRAND TOTAL		

Text B Housekeeping Development

The housekeeping development is the backbone of a hotel. The product that a hotel sells is service. So it is possible to say that a clean and attractive guest room is the product that a hotel sells. It is quite important for the housekeeping department staff to coordinate the work closely with the front office.

This department as a whole is required to make the guests' stay comfortable and pleasing. Any reasonable request must be fulfilled. Whenever and wherever possible, the staff should offer to do extra things for the guests. What is more, whenever there is an opportunity to sell the services, the staff should take it and persuade the guests to use the hotel services as much as possible. They should make sure that they are really selling what the guests wants to buy.

The housekeeping services mainly consist of chamber services and laundry services, of course including miscellaneous services. Chambermaids don't make contact with the guests very often. A chambermaid may be asked to tidy up the room at a certain time or after the guest leaves. In most cases, guests don't like to be disturbed by hanging signs on the door knob. Chambermaids also take charge of the distribution of the items supplied by the housekeeping department, such as towels, bath towels, soap, showercaps, combs, shampoo, toothpaste and so on. In some hotels, they pick up and deliver clothing for the laundry and valet service. In luxury hotels, chambermaids offer such a service that they turn down the bed covers to make the bed look more inviting. Housemen usually do heavier chores that might be considered beyond the physical capacities of women. They shampoo carpets, wash windows, remove and clean draperies, clean the public areas of the hotel, polish metal and so on. Housemen also run errands for the housekeeping department. For example, fetch something needed by the guests.

The housekeeping department also bears responsibility for the hotel laundry and valet service. It is the hotel's own work to wash hundreds or thousands of sheets, towels, tablecloths, and napkins soiled during the routine operation of the hotel. Laundry and valet service must also, of course, provide quick and efficient service for the guests who need their clothes washed, dry cleaned or pressed.

Handling lost and found articles is another service item for the housekeeping department. Guests often forget to or leave behind their personal possessions in hotel rooms. These articles may appear when the room is cleaned. Then they are turned over to the housekeeper who keep them until they are claimed or disposed of in some other way.

The housekeeping staff usually work under the supervision of the manager or an executive housekeeper. The housekeeping job is also supported by a considerable variety of materials, such as cleaning materials, bed linens, pillows, towels, paper products, matchbooks, ashtrays, stationery and so forth. These materials are quickly used up or worn out. As a result, new materials have to be ordered to replenish the stock. The housekeeping staff can do a great deal to assure a high business repeat and occupancy rate, not only through the efficiency in their jobs but also through full enthusiasm in serving guests.

Notes

1. take an opportunity 利用机会。

    eg. I take this opportunity of thanking you.（我趁此机会感谢你。）

2. miscellaneous service 各种各样的服务。

3. take charge of 负责。

    eg. Who takes charge of the task?（谁负责这项工作?）

4. valet service 旅馆中替客人洗熨衣服的人。

5. run errands for 为……跑腿。

    eg. I've no time to run errands for you.（我没有时间为你跑腿。）

6. bear responsibility for 对……负责。

7. personal possessions 个人所属物品。

8. turn over 移交。

    eg. He turned over the business to his son.（他将生意移交给了儿子。）

9. dispose of 处置

    eg. 1) How did you dispose of the matter?（你如何解决这个问题的?）

    2) He has disposed of the rubbish.（他已扔掉了垃圾。）

10. under the supervision of 在……监视下。

11. executive housekeeper 总管。

12. replenish the stock 补充库存。

    eg. You'd better replenish the fire.（你最好给火补充燃料。）

Exercises: Answer the following questions according to Text B.

1. What is the product a hotel sells?
2. What role does the front office play in the hotel service?
3. What do the housekeeping services consist of?
4. What do chambermaids mainly do?
5. What service are you getting if you have your clothes washed?
6. How do the staff devote themselves to housekeeping service?

Text C The Small Country Inn

The small country inn is just stopping place where a traveler can find food and shelter for a night or two before continuing their journey. These country inns are simple but pleasant lodgings. They do not offer the same services that hotels do. Such modern facilities as in-room televisions and telephones cannot be seen there.

Instead, they bring us the simple, natural old world charm and coziness in a scenic or historic setting. Guests might expect to find antique furniture or handmade things with folk custom. Sometimes there are as few as three or four rooms in the small country inn. Small, individually owned properties without more food and beverage and other services are able to operate with a small hotel staff possibly with just the owners themselves and a maid or two to clean guest rooms. However, guests are usually pleased with the comfort and cleanliness of accommodations and quality of the food.

The early idea of living in the small country inn was started in 1909 in Germany, by a young schoolmaster named Richard Schirrmann. Schirrmann loved the countryside around his home and spent hours exploring its beauties. He felt that his pupils, most of whom lived in the towns, should realize the wonderful scenery of the country. He began to take small groups of students on long walks through the country around his hometown, Altena.

Soon more and more students wanted to join in the traveling group. The young people, having explored the nearby regions, liked to visit more of Germany by going on longer trips. They had to find places to spend the night. The students had little money to afford to stay in expensive hotels. Thus the small country inn met their needs.

These inns are also called youth hostels. Later people from other countries recognized the advantages of this kind of travel. Soon such country inns scattered throughout some parts of the world. Now youth hostels become the international organizations, which are not run for the purpose of making money.

Of course, the small country inns are not only for young students. With the development of tourism, more and more scenic spots are explored and established in the countryside and a large number of small inns appear and flourish, which are more liked by those going off the noisy city, in search of natural beauty, peace and simple life. People can have more opportunities to enjoy the beauties of nature in a leisurely way. They are able to see places not often visited by those who travel by train, plane, or ship. The small country inns have just offered the conveniences to satisfy people's requirements.

Notes

1. 1) scatter throughout some parts of the world 分散在世界某些地方。

   2) He scattered his clothes all over the room. 房间里到处都是他的衣服。

2. enjoy the beauties of nature in a leisure way 悠闲自在地欣赏大自然美景。
3. natural old world charm and coziness 大自然古老世界的魅力和惬意。
4. antique furniture 古家具。

Exercises: Mark the following statements with "T" (True) or "F" (False) according to Text C.

1. Small country inns can not offer something to eat except the place to sleep in.
2. Schirrmann was the first man to live in the small country inn.
3. The young students could not afford to stay in expensive hotels.
4. Since there were many young students who liked to stay in small country inns, more and more inns were open to students for the purpose of making more money.
5. Small country inns provide people with opportunities to see places not often visited by those who travel by train, plane, or ship.
6. Those who don't like to live in the city have explored scenic spots and planed to move there.

Unit 6 Home Away From Home

Study structure
Text A (Intensive Reading): Home Away from Home
Dialogues
New Words and Expressions
Exercises
Text B (Extensive Reading): The International Hotel Chains
Text C (Supplementary Reading): The Cashier

Summary of the Text

Have you experience the feeling of the "home" away from home? If you have, you can really realize what an important part service quality has played in hotel operation. Then the background where the international hotel chains were formed, the development and expansion of world-famous hotel chains, and the advantages of hotel chains are respectively dealt with in Text B. Last, various items of the services from the cashier in any financial transactions are involved in this unit, too.

Text A Home Away From Home

A home can be defined as a nest or harbor where warmth, comfort, safety and conveniences can be felt. High quality of hotel services can also create a home away from home for all the traveling guests who need rest, food and drink. Hotel services should lay emphasis on conveniences, comfort, saftey, friendship, hospitality and mutual aids.

Convenience means the visible hotel facilities with practical value and complete service items, which make guests feel as if they were living in their own home.

Comfort is the quality of hotel facilities with attractive value, which makes guests feel the enjoyment combined with beauty if they live in a hotel.

Safety refers to the general hotel atmosphere and pleasant surroundings, which make guests filled with ease and pleasure and enjoy the worriless experience from "home".

Friendship can be understood as emotional services hotel staffs give with a warm, friendly and thoughtful smile, which make guests have a sentimental attachment for eastern sensibilities and human friendship.

Hospitality includes courtesy, politeness, etiquette appearance and manner that hotel staff should have. This embodies the excellent tradition of Chinese comity through services.

Mutual aid is that hotel staff should help each other to offer services at a good pace, consider guests' need as their own work aim and meanwhile provide each item of services for the guests according to certain procedure and standard. Thus guests' expenses in the hotel can be rewarded by the enjoyment with comprehensive beauty value.

Three main departments of a hotel most greatly contribute to a home feeling guests have.

The front office of a hotel is not only its "shop window" but also its "nerve center". When guests enter the hotel, they first have contact with front office workers. If they serve guests warmly, thoughtfully and politely, they will make a good impression on guests. The permanent impression is of great importance in realizing the aim of the hotel. It is within this department that the guests' vocation or business and indeed, the hotel's operation itself are made or ruined.

To fulfil these tasks, the front office staff should treat guests in good manner, serve guests with adept skill, deal with guests' complaints helpfully, and solve guests' problems efficiently. Only in this way, can guests be assured of and satisfied with other services, and really experience the warmth from "home".

Housekeeping department mainly pay more attention to the sanitation of chambers and public areas, and supply comfortable and satisfying housekeeping facilities for guests. Housekeeping income of a hotel is the key to success or failure. When guests walk into bright, clean room, they are quite pleased and feel at home. During guests' stay in the hotel, housekeeping staff should work with enthusiasm, initiative patience and thoughtfulness.

More and more hoteliers come to realize that food and beverage service is another major factor in hotel operation. In many large hotels, it brings more income than room retails. There are a number of different areas offering a variety of meals and services all within a hotel-restaurant, grill room, different bars, cafeteria and coffee shop as well as room service, lounge service and banqueting. The operation of a restaurant is a complex mixture of components in a total system. The food and beverage department involves many people working together as a team. So group cohesiveness is of particular significance there. The food and beverage department employees, especially waiters, waitresses and bartenders, can play an extremely important role in creating a pleasant atmosphere, which is one of the services our hotel sells. High quality service is dependent on the waiter and other food and beverage department staff as well, having a love for his job and a knowledge of its working right down to the last detail. The initial contact with the customer matters greatly. A good waiter tries to satisfy the requirements of both the customer and the restaurant at once. A cordial smile, plenty of courtesy with sincere effort and efficiency will bring more guests "home".

It is the tendency of modern hotel development for guests to enjoy homelike services. Hotel staff should throw themselves into their work heart and soul. They should treat guests as friends, relatives and thought about them in all respects. The charm of serving with feelings makes many guests become voluntary propagandists, which has more effects on hotel business than advertisements. There will be more and more guests who would like to stay in the home away from home.

Dialogues

Dialogue A: An announcement to leave the hotel

A. I'll check out at about 1:00 p.m.
B. Can you vacate your room right now?
A. Then can I deposit my things here if I vacate the room right now?
B. Certainly.
A. No, I can't. I'll be busy until one o'clock because it'll take me some time to pack the things.
B. I'm afraid you'll be charged half the price for one night.
A. What? Additional payment? I didn't arrive here until a little past two early in the morning.
B. You are right. But one arrives at the hotel before 5 a.m. just as he does the night before the day.
A. How strange it seems to have to vacate the room before noon.
B. Sorry, everyone is expected to check out before 12:00.

Dialogue B: Checking out

A. Hello, this is William Cotton in Room 427. I'd like to check out.
B. Just a moment, please. I'll draw up your bill for you... Your bill totals $350.

A. Let me see it. OK. Here is ＄400.

B. Here is your ＄50 change. Thank you for your coming here. Hope to see you again.

A. Thanks. Please write two receipts since meals are paid by myself and the fee for the room is paid by the company.

B. OK. Wait a moment, please.

A. Sorry, Mr. Cotton. I've kept you wait so long. Please sign your name on the receipt.

New Words and Expressions

1. hospitality /ˌhɔspiˈtæliti/ n. 好客,殷勤
2. visible /ˈvizəbl/ adj. 看得见的
3. villa /ˈvilə/ n. 别墅
4. combine /kəmˈbain/ vt. 使结合
5. ease /iːz/ n. 舒适,安逸,自在
6. sentimental /ˌsentiˈmentl/ adj. 感伤的,多愁善感的
7. attachment /əˈtætʃmənt/ n. 依恋,附属品
8. sensibility /ˌsensiˈbiliti/ n. 情感,感情,敏感
9. courtesy /ˈkəːtəsi/ n. 礼貌,谦恭
10. etiquette /ˈetiket/ n. 礼节,礼仪
11. embody /imˈbɔdi/ vt. 体现
12. comity /ˈkɔmiti/ n. 礼让
13. pace /peis/ n. 步速,速度,步态
14. procedure /prəˈsiːdʒə/ n. 程序,步骤
15. comprehensive /ˌkɔmpriˈhensiv/ adj. 理解的
16. nerve /nəːv/ n. 神经
17. impression /ˈimˈpreʃən/ n. 印象
18. permanent /ˈpəːmənənt/ adj. 永久的
19. adept /ˈædept/ adj. 内行的,熟练的
20. complaint /kəmˈpleint/ n. 抱怨,投诉
21. efficiently /iˈfiʃəntli/ adv. 有效地
22. assure /əˈʃuə/ vt. 使确信,使放心
23. sanitation /ˌsæniˈteiʃən/ n. 卫生
24. enthusiasm /inˈθjuːziæszəm/ n. 热情
25. initiative /iˈniʃiətiv/ n. 主动性

26. hotelier /həu'telei/ n. 旅馆老板
27. retail /'riteil/ n. 零售
28. grill /gril/ n. 烤架,烧烤
29. cafeteria /kæfi'tiəriə/ n. 自助食堂
30. lounge /laundʒ/ n. (旅馆的)休息室
31. banquet /'bæŋkwit/ n. 宴会
32. complex /'kɔmpleks/ adj. 复杂的
33. component /kəm'pɒnnənt/ n. 组成部分
34. cohesiveness /kəu'hi:siv/ n. 粘和,紧密结合在一起
35. bartender /'ba:tendə/ n. 酒吧招待员
36. atmosphere /'ætəməsfiə/ n. 气氛
37. cordial /'kɔ:djəl/ adj. 热诚的
38. charm /tʃa:m/ n. 魅力
39. voluntary /'vɔlɔntəri/ adj. 自愿的
40. propagandist /prɔpə'gændist/ n. 宣传员
41. vacate /və'keit/ vt. 腾出,空出
42. deposit /di'pɔzit/ vt. 存放
43. draw up 写出,草拟
44. mutual aid 相互帮助

Notes

1. lay emphasis on 指将重点放在……。

   eg. Our government lays emphasis on the development of economy. (我们的政府着重发展经济。)

2. combine...with 使相结合。

   eg. Theory must be combined with practice. (理论必须与实践相结合。)

3. have a sentimental attachment for 对……留恋。

4. at a good pace 快速地。

   eg. Tourism has been developed at a good pace. (旅游业已快速发展。)

5. make a good impression on 给……留下好印象。

6. contribute to 有助于,起一份作用。

   eg. Such medicine contributes greatly to his disease. (这种药对他的病很有作用。)

7. throw oneself into one's work heart and soul 全身心地投入到工作中。

8. in all respects 在各个方面。

Useful Expressions and Patterns

1) I'd like to settle my bill.
   我想结账。

2) Please make up my bill to May 6th.
   请给我结账到 5 月 6 日。

3) I'd like to use a safety deposit box.
   我想使用保险柜。

4) Would you like to deposit or withdraw something?
   您要存放还是提取什麽?

5) If you would like to use the contents during the period of use, please come here in person. After confirming your signature, we will open the box.
   使用本柜期间,您若想取用里面的东西,请亲自来,待确认您的签名之后,我们才开柜。

6) How much do you charge for a double room for a night?
   你们对双人房间一晚收费多少?

7) Is there a discount for company booking?
   团体订房间可以打折扣么?

8) You don't have to pay now. The laundry will be debited to your bill.
   您现在不用付款,洗衣费将计到您的账单上。

9) I'll get the porter to bring down your luggage soon.
   我会让行李员将您的行李很快搬下来。

10. He has vacated the rented house.
    所租的房屋他已空出来了。

11. —I'd like to confirm the room charge per night.
    —The rate is ＄32.00 for each night plus tax and service change.
    ——我想知道每天的房租是多少?
    ——房租每晚 32 美元,税款和服务费另加。

12. Miss, I want to check out. Will you please have the bill ready for me? I'll come down in a few minutes.
    小姐,我要结账,请把账单准备好,我一会就下来。

Exercises

I. Answer the following questions according to Text A.
1. Why is a hotel called a home away from home?
2. What does hospitality include?
3. What influence does the front office of a hotel have on guests?
4. How do the front office staff serve guests?
5. What should the housekeeping department lay emphasis on?
6. Why is food and beverage service another important factor in hotel operation?
7. What is high quality service like in the food and beverage department?
8. What has more effects on hotel business than advertisement?

II. Mark the following statements with "T" (True) or "F" (False) according to Text A.
1. Conveniences and comfort are regarded as the most important factor in hotel operation.
2. Safety is not included in hotel services because it is the police's task to protect people from being harmed.
3. What makes guests have a sentimental attachment for a hotel is the warm, friendly and thoughtful services.
4. The front office is much more important than housekeeping department because it is the nerve center of a hotel.
5. The quality of housekeeping service is greatly concerned with guests' homelike feeling.
6. Hotel staff must try to satisfy as many requirements from the customers as possible if they want to create a good image.

III. Translation.
1. Translate the following sentences into Chinese.
1) The employee who checks in arriving guests and assigns them to their rooms is the room clerk.
2) When the room clerk has confirmed the availability of the accommodations, the guest fills out a registration card with his name, home address, and any other pertinent information.
3) A guide has a prepared talk during which he gives information about the sights that will be visited, but he must also be able to answer questions and to deal with

the human problems that may arise.

4) Tourist must fill out a "Baggage Declaration for Passengers". The copy of "Baggage Declaration for Passengers" must be kept and submitted for customs inspection on leaving China.

5) All hotel staff ought to remember that the hotel will enjoy greater financial success only with the greater satisfaction the guests receive from the "home away from home".

6) A tourism information office promotes, or builds travel to a destination country through advertising and special promotional activities.

2. Translate the following into English.
1) 我特别想成为一名职业的酒店管理人员。
2) 您能不能给我安排一个客房服务员工作?
3) 我在酒店管理方面得过学位,还修过计算机课程。
4) 委托经营(management)是指连锁饭店与饭店拥有者签订合同。
5) 其他在世界范围内经营业务的有"喜来登"(Sheraton)、"洲际"(Inter-Continental)、"福特信托"(Trust Houses)、"希而顿国际"(Hilton International)和"拉马达"(Romada Inns)等连锁旅馆公司。
6) 宾客在宾馆收银台兑换一些货币并办理结账。

IV. Complete the following dialogue.

Scene: Mr. Wang checks out at the cashier's desk.

Cashier = C   Mr. Wang = W

C: Good afternoon, Sir. What _____ I _____ for you?

W: I want to _____ out today.

C: _____ me _____ _____ number, please. And you want to _____ now?

W: Yes, my room is 1205.

C: Just a _____, please. Are you Mr. Wang Lin _____ Room 1205?

W: Yes.

C: Mr. Wang, these are the bills you _____ in _____ departments in our hotel. Please check _____ and I'll _____ a bill of your total _____ and a receipt.

W: No problem.

C: How _____ _____ _____ _____ _____, Mr. Wang?

W: Master Card. Here are the card and my I.D.

C: Sorry to have kept you _____, Mr. Wang. Here are your bill and receipt. I hope you _____ here and have _____ trip home.

W: Thank you.

V. Vocabulary and Structure.

1. Fill in the blank with the words or expressions given below. Change the form where necessary.

   | mutual; embody; lay emphasis on; at a good pace; have a sentimental attachment for; adept; be assure of; make an impression on; etiquette; contribute to |

   1) The students' performance _____ deep _____ the guests.
   2) Diplomatic _____ is quite necessary in dealing with foreign affairs.
   3) The close relationship between friends results from the _____ understanding.
   4) The factory has produced the exported goods _____.
   5) Guests _____ the considerate services of the hotel.
   6) The patient has been _____ the safety of the operation.
   7) The improvement of traffic facilities _____ greatly _____ the development of tourist industry.
   8) My uncle is _____ in treating such disease.
   9) The school has always _____ great _____ the teaching of basic subjects.
   10) Package tour _____ the advantage of low expense and more convenience.

2. Match the following two columns.

   A. view the scenery   a. 方便进入景点
   B. accommodation and support facilities   b. 有导游的旅游
   C. easy access to resorts   c. 旺季/淡季
   D. cultural visit   d. 10 日游
   E. guided tour   e. 零售业务
   F. high/low season   f. 赏景
   G. 10-Day Excursions   g. 旅行代理商
   H. retail business   h. 住宿及其他辅助设施
   I. travel agents   i. 旅游宣传册
   J. Tour Brochure   j. 文化旅游

3. Multiple Choice.

   1) The city has taken the _____ in banning smoking in public.
      A. initiate   B. initiative
      C. initial   D. initiation
   2) Foreign investment in recent years have _____ the growth of the local economy.

A. arisen   B. risen
C. accelerated   D. gone

3) I'll feel more _____ with a burglar alarm.
   A. secure   B. safe
   C. easy   D. comfortable

4) It is unsafe for a traveller to carry a large amount of _____.
   A. cashier   B. cast
   C. coin   D. cash

5) _____ is the largest chain in the word, with more than 350,000 units in about 1900 properties.
   A. Hilton Hotel   B. City Hotel
   C. Holiday Inn   D. Tremont House

6) China now ranked _____ in the world in terms of tourism dollars.
   A. sixth   B. tenth
   C. ninth   D. fifth

7) As a salesman, he works on a _____ basis.
   A. commission   B. commercial
   C. committee   D. income

8) When new housing is being built, _____ is one of the first things to consider.
   A. health   B. clean
   C. sanitation   D. surroundings

9) He _____ all his accounts before leaving the deluxe hotel.
   A. solve   B. settled
   C. take   D. count

10) Short of capital was a factor _____ economic development.
    A. helping   B. preventing
    C. holding out   D. holding back

VI. Situational Dialogue.

Make up a dialogue according to the given situation:

This is the conversation between Cashier and Guest. The guest wants to leave the hotel one day earlier. But he wants to make up his bill to the planned day. The cashier draws up his bill for him, tells him the total number of money he should pay for the items of services, and asks him how he would like to make the payment. The guest pays his bill in cash. The cashier wants the guest to check the bill, gives back change and receipt, and hope to see the guest again.

VII. Mini Dialogues.

Dialogues A: Checking out

A: Operator, connect me with the cashier please?

A: Miss, I want to check out. Will you please have the bill ready for me? I'll come down in a few minutes.

C: OK. Sir. I'll bill you right away.

A: Operator, sorry to bother you again. Will you please send me a porter to carry my luggage downstairs?

Dialogues B: Changing some money

A: I'd like to change some money. What's the exchange rate today?

B: According to the present rate, it's 8.74 yuan to the dollar.

A: How much would you like to change?

B: 700 U.S. dollars. By the way, will you please give me in ones or fives? I need some small changes.

A: Here is your money. Please count them.

Dialogues C: Depositing valuables

A: Excuse me. Can I deposit valuables here?

B: Of course, you can. Please put your articles in this bag and seal it.

A: OK.

B: How long would you like us to keep them?

A: Till Friday when I check out.

VIII. Practical Writing: Fill in the registration form of temporary residence.

Text B The International Hotel Chains

Changes have constantly taken place in the lodging industry with the development of science and technology, which brings more conveniences to meet the needs and expectations of travelers. However, economical recessions, energy crisis, periods of accelerating inflation, skilled labor shortages, low productivity, severe overbuilding, competition, foreign exchange fluctuations and numerous ownership changes have all had an impact on hotel occupancy rates and profitability at some time. These terrible cases have never held back but promoted the progress of the lodging industry.

For centuries, the hotel business was run as privately owned, independent enterprises. The Caesar Ritz group was successfully developed and grown up. Ritz usually let an employee appoint and oversee the managers of separately owned hotels. That arrangement was made by the hotel management contract several years later. According to the contract, the owners of a hotel plant manage the establishment, which is one of the methods through which hotel chains have grown in recent years. Other hotels were allowed to advertise themselves as branches of a Ritz hotel. The Ritz chain reached its peak near the end of the nineteenth century with luxury hotels set up in many major European cities and the other parts of the world such as Cairo, Johannesburg and New York. Today the Ritz name still symbolizes luxury and first-class service.

It was E. M Statler that became one of the first hotel chains in the modern sense. Beginning with one hotel in 1901, the Statler enterprise was eventually enlarged to a chain of ten major hotels. Statler was the first to point out the economic and financial advantages of operating several large hotels under a single management. He was able to get more profits from centralizing purchasing, cost control and marketing. Most of his hotels have similar name, style and size. However, the chain concept was slowly spread because of two world wars and even hotel chain operators were looked down on. Conrad Hilton contributed greatly to the popularity and operation of international hotel chains. Conrad Hilton is especially considered as the originator of the hotel management contract. Kemmons Wilson and Wallace John, who established Holiday Inn, fully capitalized on the chain concept by franchising the Holiday Inn name and made a national reservation net work available. Franchising was another way to the growth of hotel chains, which permitted an enterprise to operate under a corporate name and usually with standards established by the licensing corporation, and many hotel and motel companies followed this method, especially in the budget category.

There are several other methods to expand hotel chains. One is to invest money directly. The head corporation itself puts up the necessary fund to build and operate a new hotel or to buy and refurbish an old one. Another is by establishing management contracts, under which, the chain is run in its own ways and gets a percentage of profits. Joint venture is similar to management contracts and it's partnership business, in which both the chain and local partners make a joint investment for new construction or the purchase of an existing building. Franchising is another way widely used by some motel chains. Operators can use the plans, manuals of procedure and advertising materials, and get a great deal of help from the licensing corporation by paying a fee and putting up the capital.

Hotel chains have many competitive advantages over individually owned establishments. Firstly, they don't need to spend much money on advertising, which is too expensive for individual hotel operators. The advertising and public-relation professionals from the chains' headquarters are engaged in publicity work. Secondly the chains have the standardization of equipment and operating procedures. A very visible degree of uniformity between the chain hotels can be reflected in some tasks. Thirdly, the most important and most obvious advantage is the increased efficiency in making and controlling reservations. Hotel chains can make it easy for travellers to reserve rooms and flights in a minute by telephone and computer. For instance, it is possible for a guest to confirm space while he or she is still on the phone. Fourthly, hotel chains have increased sales potential for conventions. With the chains spread in different parts of the country, the sponsoring group can hold its meetings in one location one year and another the next and get similar service and costs. Fifthly, hotel chains are superior in planning and designing hotels for they have access to expensive market research data on site selection and size of the hotel. Sixthly, chain system plays an important role by increasing the efficiency of the whole organization in other ways. For example, it can buy many kinds of equipment and supplies in large quantities. The accounting and auditing systems of the chains can be centralized. A centralized personnel office for managerial and technical positions throughout the chain also provides an advantage in securing competent people. The headquarters have the opportunity to make their own staff trained in member hotels and the management trainees will gain the necessary expertise in some aspects in order to direct and train others.

The early American chains, such as Hilton and Inter-Continental were able to get more profits at low risk. But now American chains face a barrage of European and Asian hotel chains which can match them in service standards as the market is becoming more and more competitive.

However, American lodging industry is still in the dominating position. Of the top 50 hotel chains in the world, 25 have their headquarters in the USA. But European and Asian companies are catching up with American companies in management and service quality.

Note

1. constantly 始终,不断地
   eg. The smelly air makes us breathless and cough constantly.(难闻的空气使我们窒息,不断地咳嗽。)

2. recession 衰退,暴跌
   eg. It's a recession when your neighbour loses his job; it's a depression when you loses your own.(邻居失业意味着经济萧条,自己失业意味着意志消沉。)

3. accelerate 加速
   eg. Fertilizer will accelerate the growth of these tomato plants.(化肥加速了这些西红柿苗的生长。)

4. inflation 通货膨胀
   eg. Economic depression leads to inflation.(经济萧条导致通货膨胀。)

5. severe 严重的
   eg. She has only just recovered from a severe illness.(他刚从严重的疾病中康复。)

6. fluctuation 涨落,波动
   eg. The fluctuations of prices have great effects on business.(价格的波动对生意有很大影响。)

7. have an impact on 对……有影响
   eg. That book had(made) a great impact on its readers.(那本书对它的读者有很大影响。)

8. occupancy 占据,占有

9. profitability 利益,有利可图

10. hold back 妨碍,阻碍
    eg. Shortage of capital was a factor holding back economic development.(缺乏资金是妨碍经济发展的一个因素。)

11. enterprise 企业

12. appoint 任命,委任
    eg. They appointed him (to be) manager.(他们任命他为经理。)

13. oversee 监督,监视
    eg. He oversaw the building of the bridge.(他曾监管那座桥的建设。)

14. contract 合同

15. reach its peak 达到顶峰

16. luxury 豪华,奢侈

    eg. They led a life of luxury.（他过着奢侈的生活。）

17. symbolize 象征着

    eg. The dove symbolizes peace.（鸽子象征和平。）

18. centralizing purchasing 购买权集中

19. concept 概念

20. spread 传播,散布

    eg. Television is a very efficient medium for spreading information.（电视是传播信息的有效媒介。）

21. originator 创始者

22. capitalize on 利用

    eg. capitalize on the opponent's mistakes（利用对手的错误）

23. franchise 给……以特许

24. corporate 共同的,全体的

25. refurbish 更新

    eg. You'd better refurbish the old house.（你最好将那旧房屋刷新一下。）

26. Joint venture 合资

27. manual 手册,指南

28. licensing corporation 授权公司

29. professional 专业人员

30. headquarter 总部

31. be engaged in publicity work 从事宣传工作

32. uniformity 一致性

33. sponsoring group 赞助团体

34. have access to 进入,享用

    eg. The poor children had no access to education.（那些穷孩子过去没有受教育的机会。）

35. accounting and auditing 财会和审记

36. in securing competent people 在获得有能力人才方面

37. trainee 受训练人

38. expertise 专门知识

    eg. It's important for him to have the expertise in the field.（具备那方面的专业知识对他来说很重要。）

39. a barrage of 接二连三地猛击

    eg. a barrage of questions（连珠炮似的问题）

40. in the dominating position 处于支配性位置

Exercises: Answer the following questions according to Text B.
1. What promotes the beginning of hotel chains?
2. How many chain hotels have been mentioned in the passage? What are they?
3. In what ways are hotel chains expanded?
4. How many competitive advantages over individually owned establishment do hotel chains have?
5. Why do hotel chains get more profits from the sale of convention hotels?
6. Why do we say that the lodging industry in the U.S.A is still in the first place?

Text C   The Cashier

The cashier transacts the business of money involved in the bank, store, hotel and other units. Regardless of whether the guest or customer will use cash, a check, a credit card or other forms of defrayment, the eventual payment should be ensured.

When you use notes and coins, the money is called cash. You can get change from the cashier if you pay for something. Change means smaller notes or coins instead of a large note or coin. Sometimes you also need to walk to the cashier directly to make change. The cashier helps you to cash a cheque when you give the cheque to the bank and receive the same amount in notes and coins. The special cheques used for travelling abroad are called traveller's cheques; The cashier can also cash traveller's cheques for you. Western people are not accustomed to carrying cash with them. Often it is not safe or convenient to have large amounts of cash on hand. Most people use checks and credit cards to avoid having heavy cash. Checks are commonly used to pay rent, utilities and telephone bills. There are personal checks issued by banks. A person will deposit money in a checking account. The bank will give him/her special pieces of paper on which to write checks. People use the check to replace cash. Usually the cashier, the person accepting the check will ask the person writing the check for identification: eg. a driver's license, passport, university identification card. If a person wrtite checks for more money than has been deposited in the bank, the person has overdrawn the account. There are penalties for overdrawing an account.

Credit cards are made of pieces of plastic, which are issued by the banks or stores and encourge people to spend more money. Sometimes university bookstores also frequently issue credit cards to graduate students and visiting scholars. When purchasing something, the buyer will give his credit card to the cashier of the store. The cashier will get information from the credit card, and accept it instead of money. The cashier will give the buyer a receipt. Another receipt is presented to the bank, which will then bill the buyer, usually after 30 years.

The cashier also deals with foreign currency exchange. Currency means varieties of money belonging to different countries. If you buy a different currency by selling yours, you are exchanging money. When you are changing money in the United states, you should know how much your currency costs for 1 dollar. The price is called the rate of exchange. Each time you exchange money, the cashier will ask you for a small charge as commission. A lot of money will be lost in the exchanging process as fees are changed. The less you exchange, the more obvious it is. As a result, it's cheaper to exchange several notes together than to exchange one at a time. If you are going to exchange money at a bank, make sure of the exchange rate first. In addition to the exchange counters in the bank, there are exchange counters in some major stores to make overseas tourist feel convenient.

The cashier is also involved in hotel accounting when guests want to check out. Guests bills must be posted or entered on his or her account as soon as possible. In addition to the charge for the guest's room, there may also be the fees for telephone, the laundry service, the restaurant and room service. All the financial transactions not only must be posted but also must be checked for accuracy. It is the night auditor's job to go through this mass of figures on the night shift. At that time, there is little business in the hotel.

The cashier handles financial matters for the customers at the front desk, including receiving payment for bills, making change and exchanging foreign currency. When listing a guest's bill, the cashier will check if a reservation deposit has been paid. If it has, the amount of the deposit will be deducted from the bill. The cashier will find out if you are entitled to any kind of discount or complimentary rate. If you are, the cashier will make necessary reduction. The cashier will also remind you to return your room key to the reception desk before you leave the hotel. If you settle your account in traveler's checks, the cashier will make sure that you countersign the check in front of them. They won't accept checks that have already been countersigned.

A cashier must be responsible for the business when doing financial calculations. Careless mistakes will bring great loss to both customers and business organizations.

Notes

1. cashier 出纳员
2. transact 处理,办理

    eg. They transacted most of their business by phone.（他们大多数生意都是通电话进行的。）
3. regardless of 不管,不顾

    eg. Regardless of wind and rain, he does exercise every day.（不管风和雨,他每天都锻炼。）
4. defrayment 支付
5. ensure 使确信,保证,担保

    eg. He can't ensure that the defrayment will be there in time.（他不能保证及时付款。）
6. notes 纸币、票据
7. cash a cheque 兑换支票
8. amount 数量
9. be accustomed to 习惯于……

    eg. We are not accustomed to the hot weather here.（我们不习惯这儿的天气。）
10. on hand

    eg. They have a large stock on hand.（他们手头有大批存货。）
11. utilities 公用事业
12. issue 问题
13. deposit money in a checking account 用支票账户存钱
14. write checks 开支票
15. university identification card 学生证
16. overdraw the account 透支账户

    eg. You have to deposit more money in the bank to avoid overdrawing the account.（你得在银行多存钱才能避免透支。）
17. penalty 处罚、罚款
18. bill the buyer 给顾客开账单
19. make change 找零钱
20. commission 佣金,回扣

    eg. Your commission is 10% of the quoted gross rate.（你可以得到报价总

额 10%的回扣。)
21. hotel accounting 宾馆账目
22. auditor 审计员
23. on the day/night shift 值白/夜班

    eg. Are you on the day shift or on the night shift today?（你今天值白班还是夜班？）
24. deduct 扣除，减去

    eg. Nowadays income tax is normally deducted from a person's wages.（现在正常要从个人工资中扣除收入税。）
25. discount 折扣
26. entitle 给……权利，给予

    eg. 1) His high score entitled him to a prize.（他的高分使他有获奖权。）

    2) If you fail three times, you are not entitled to try any more.（如果你失败三次，你就无权再试了。）
27. complimentary 免费的

    eg. Have you got the complimentary ticket to the film?（你有看电影的免费入场券吗？）
28. settle one's account 结账
29. countersign 会签，确认

Exercises: Mark the following statements with "T"(True) or "F"(False) according to Text C.

1. The cashier only deals with the business related to the money in the bank.
2. Most western people use checks or credit cards while travelling because it is unsafe to carry heavy cash with them.
3. A person may write checks for more money than that deposited in the bank.
4. By using credit cards, a person can buy as many things as he or she likes to.
5. Since fees are charged when you deal with foreign currency exchange, it is better to exchange more notes together than to exchange one at a time.
6. When you settle your account, a reservation deposit will also be added to your bill.

Unit 7　Typical Chinese Cuisine

Study structure

Text A (Intensive Reading): Chinese Cuisine
Dialogues
New Words and Expressions
Exercises
Text B (Extensive Reading): Different Table Manners Between Chinese and Westerners
Text C (Supplementary Reading): How to Cook Mapo Beancurd

Summary of the Text

　　This unit deals with the best-known features of Chinese cuisine in Text A, including main features, basic cooking techniques, and typical menu items of eight styles of regional dishes, different table manners between Chinese and Westerners in Text B, and the culinary art of a famous Sichuan dish— Mapo Beancurd in Text C.

Text A　Chinese Cuisine

　　Chinese Cuisine is famous all over the world for its fantastic flavor and delicate techniques. Today it is widely accepted that it can be divided into eight styles of regional dishes although there are many other famous local dishes, such as Beijing dishes and Shanghai dishes.

Shandong Cuisine

　　Consisting of Jinan cuisine and Jiaodong cuisine, Shandong cuisine, clean, pure and not greasy, is characterized by its emphasis on aroma, freshness, crispness and tenderness. Fistulous onion and garlic are frequently used as seasonings in Shandong dishes. The main cooking techniques include quick frying, quick frying with corn flour, stew braising, roasting, boiling and crystallizing with honey.

　　Typical menu items are Fried Sea Cucumber with Fistulous Onion, Yellow River Carp in Sweet and Sour sauce, Braised Abalone with Shells.

Sichuan Cuisine

Sichuan dishes are one of the most famous dishes in China. Characterized by its spicy and pungent flavors, Sichuan cuisine, with a myriad of tastes, emphasizes the use of chili and Pepper powder. Garlic, ginger and fermented soybean are also used in the cooking process. Wild edible herbs and the meat of domestic animals and birds are often chosen as ingredients. The cooking techniques include sauting, quick frying, dry frying, pickling and so on.

Typical menu items are Gongbao Diced Chicken, Twice Cooked Pork, Mapo Beancurd.

Guangdong Cuisine (Cantonese Cuisine)

Consisting of Cantonese, Chaozhou and Dongjiang cuisine, Cantonese cuisine is renowned for its fresh materials and great tenderness. Seafood, fresh water fish and fowl are usually cooked as main ingredients in Cantonese dishes. The basic cooking techniques include roasting, stir-frying, sauting, deep-frying, braising, stewing and steaming. Steaming and stir-frying are most frequently used to preserve the ingredients' natural flavors. Guangdong chefs also pay much attention to the artistic presentation of their dishes.

Typical menu items are Shark Fin Soup, Cantonese Fried Pigeon, and Beef Slices with Oyster Sauce.

Fujian Cuisine

Composed of Fuzhou cuisine, Quanzhou cuisine and Xiamen cuisine, Fujian cuisine is famous for its choice of seafood, beautiful color and "pickled taste".

Typical menu items are Buddha Jumping Over the Wall, and Prawn with Dragon's Body and Phoenix's tail.

Hunan Cuisine

Hunan cuisine consists of local dishes of Xiangjiang River area, Dongting Lake area and Western Hunan coteau areas. It is characterized by thick and pungent flavors. Chili, pepper and shallot are usually necessities in Hunan dishes.

Typical menu items are Dong'an Fledgling Chicken, Hot-Spiced and Peppered Fledgling Chicken, and Steamed Peckled Meat.

Huaiyang Cuisine

Huaiyang cuisine, also called Jiangsu cuisine, mainly consist of Yangzhou, Zhenjiang, and Huaian cuisine originated in villages south of the Yangtze River. It is renowned not only for its material selection but for the fine workmanship in cutting, matching, cooking, and arranging. The cooking techniques of it include stewing, braising, roasting, and simmering. The flavor of Huaiyang cuisine is light, fresh and sweet and its presentation is delicately elegant.

Typical menu items are Squirrel with Mandarin Fish, Crystal Meat, and Crisp Eel.

Zhejiang Cuisine

Composed of local dishes of Hangzhou, Ningbo, and Shaoxing, Zhejiang cuisine wins its reputation for freshness, tenderness, softness, and smoothness of its dishes with their mellow fragrance. Hangzhou cuisine is the most famous one of the three.

Typical menu items are West Lake Vinegar Fish, Longjing Shelled Shrimp, and Beggar's Chicken.

Anhui Cuisine

Anhui cuisine focus much more attention on the temperature in cooking and Anhui chefs are good at braising and stewing. Often ham will be added to improve taste and rock candy can be added to gain freshness.

Typical menu items are Smoked Chicken With Tea, and Huangshan Braised Pigeon.

New Words and Expressions

1. cuisine   /kwiˈziːn/   n. 烹调(法)
2. flavor   /ˈfleivə/   n.(独特的)味道,(包括不同味道的)风味
3. technique   /tekˈniːk/   n. 技艺, 技巧, 技术
4. greasy   /ˈgriːzi/   adj. 油腻的, 脂肪多的
5. characterize   /ˈkærəktəraiz/   v. 具有……的特征/特性/特色
6. aroma   /əˈrəumə/   n. 香味, 芳香, 香气
7. fistulous onion   /ˈfistjuləsˈʌniən/   n. 大葱
8. garlic   /ˈgaːlik/   n. 大蒜

9.	stew	/stju:/	v. 以文火煮、炖、烩
10.	braise	/breiz/	v. (用文火)焖
11.	crystallize	/ˈkristəlaiz/	v. 1.将(水果)浸糖 2.使……结晶
12.	abalone	/ˌæbəˈləuni/	n. 鲍鱼
13.	spicy	/ˈspaisi/	adj. 辛辣的,芳香的,加有香料的
14.	pungent	/ˈpʌndʒənt/	adj. 味道刺激性强的,辛辣的,刺鼻的
15.	myriad	/ˈmiriəd/	n. 无数,众多
16.	ginger	/ˈdʒindʒə/	n. 姜
17.	ferment	/ˈfə:ment/	v. 发酵
18.	soybean	/ˈsɔibi:n/	n. 大豆
19.	edible	/ˈedibl/	adj. 可食的,食用的
20.	herb	/hə:b/	n. 草,药草
21.	ingredient	/inˈgri:djənt/	n. 成分,原料,材料
22.	saute	/ˈsəutei/	v.n. 嫩煎
23.	fowl	/foul/	n. 家禽,鸡肉,鸟肉
24.	chef	/ʃef/	n. 厨师,主厨,大师傅
25.	prawn	/prɔ:n/	n. 对虾
26.	coteau	/kɔuˈtəu/	n. 丘陵地,高地
27.	shallot	/ʃəˈlɔt/	n. 冬葱,青葱
28.	fledgling	/ˈfledʒliŋ/	n. 刚长毛的(刚会飞的)雏鸟
29.	originate	/ɔˈridʒəneit/	v. 开始,创造出,产生出
30.	simmer	/ˈsimə/	v. 煨
31.	mellow	/ˈmeləu/	adj. 甜而多汁的,芳醇的
32.	vinegar	/ˈvinigə/	n. 醋
33.	shelled	/ʃeld/	adj. 脱壳的,去壳的
34.	divide into		把……分成
35.	consist of		由……组成/构成
36.	be characterized by		具有……的特征/特性
37.	originate in/ from		产生于,发祥于

Notes

1. quick fry 爆
2. quick fry with corn flour 熘
3. stew brais 扒
4. roast 烤

5. boil 煮

6. crystallize with honey 蜜

7. Fried Sea Cucumber with Fistulous Onion 葱烧海参

8. Yellow River Carp in Sweet and Sour Sauce 糖醋黄河鲤鱼

9. Braised Abalone with Shells 生焖鲍鱼

10. dry fry 干煸

11. pickle 腌

12. Gongbao Diced Chicken 宫保鸡丁

13. Twice Cooked Pock 回锅肉

14. Mapo Beancurd 麻婆豆腐

15. stir-fry 炒

16. deep-fry 炸

17. steam 蒸

18. Shark Fin Soup 鱼翅汤

19. Beef Sliced with Oyster Sauce 蚝油牛肉

20. Cantonese Fried Pigeon 脆皮乳鸽

21. Buddha Jumping Over the Wall 佛跳墙

22. Prawn with Dragon's Body and Phoenix's Tail 龙身凤尾虾

23. Dong'an Fledgling Chicken 东安子鸡

24. Hot-Spiced and Peppered Fledgling Chicken 麻辣童子鸡

25. Steamed Pickled Meat 蒸腊肉

26. Squirrel with Mandarin Fish 松鼠鳜鱼

27. Crystal Meat 水晶肉

28. Crisp Eel 脆皮鳝鱼

29. West Lake Vinegar Fish 西湖醋鱼

30. Longjing Shelled Shrimp 龙井虾仁

31. Beggar's Chicken 叫化鸡

32. rock candy 冰糖

33. Smoked Chicken with Tea 茶叶熏鸡

34. Huangshan Braised Pigeon 黄山炖鸽

Dialogues

Dialogue A: A Private Room for Eight

A = Attendant   G = Guest

A: This is Spring Restaurant. Good morning. Can I help you?

G: I'd like to reserve a private room for eight people this evening.

A: Certainly. When are you coming?

G: About 7:00 p.m.

A: May I have your name, sir, please?

G: Please book it under the name of Mr. White. And can you tell me the name of room?

A: We will arrange the room "Rainbow" for you. And do you want to order now?

G: No. We'll order in the evening.

A: Is there anything else you would like us to prepare?

G: No, thank you.

A: You're welcome. See you then.

G: See you.

Dialogue B: Ordering Steak

W = Waiter   G = Guest

W: May I take your order, sir?

G: Yes, I will have steak.

W: How would you like your steak done, rare, medium, or well done?

G: I'd like rare, please.

W: What would you like to go with your steak?

G: Pea and carrots.

W: Mashed, baked or boiled potato?

G: A baked potato, please.

W: Would you care for a salad, sir?

G: Yes. Could you make some recommendations?

W: How about a mixed vegetable salad or a sliced tomato salad?

G: A sliced tomato salad would be fine.

Notes

1. rare 嫩的
2. medium 半熟
3. well done 熟透
4. mashed 捣成糊的
5. mashed potato 土豆泥
6. baked 烤的

7. boiled 煮的
8. mixed vegetable salad 什锦蔬菜沙拉
9. sliced tomato salad 番茄沙拉

Useful Expressions and Patterns

1. I'd like to book a table for four this evening.
   我要订一张四人桌,今晚用。

2. When are you coming?
   您什么时候来?

3. When would you like your table?
   您什么时候来就餐?

4. When should we expect you, sir?
   我们什么时间恭候您,先生?

5. May/Can I take your order now?
   现在可以请您点菜了吗?

6. How would you like your steak done?
   您的牛排要多大火候的?

7. How do you like your steak cooked?
   您的牛排要做到什么火候?

8. What woulk you like to go with your steak?
   您的牛排要配什么蔬菜啊?

9. Would you care for a salad, sir?
   您要不要来份沙拉,先生?

10. Can/Could you make some recommendations?
    你能给推荐一下吗?

11. How about...?
    ……怎么样?

12. Our specialties are...
    我们的特色菜有……

Exercises

I. Answer the following questions according to text A.

1. What are the qualities of Chinese cuisine?
2. How many famous styles of dishes are there in China?

3. What are the features of Shandong cuisine?
4. Can you tell any famous Sichuan dishes?
5. What does Zhejiang dishes consist of?

II. **Mark the following statements with "T"(Ture) or "F"(False) according to Text A.**

1. Huaiyang Cuisine is also called Jiangsu Cuisine.
2. Buddha Jumping Over the Wall is a Sichuan dish.
3. Chili, pepper and shallot are usually necessities in Guangdong dishes.
4. Beijing dishes and Shanghai dishes are also very famous.
5. Guangdong chefs pay much attention to the artistic presentation of their dishes.
6. West Lake Vinegar Fish is a Huaiyang dish.
7. Smoked Chicken With Tea is a Hunan dish.
8. Fistulous Onion is often used in Anhui cuisine.

III. **Translation.**

1. Tanslate the following sentences into Chinese.
1) Chinese Cuisin is famous all over the world for its fantastic flavor and delicate techniques.
2) Consisting of Jinan cuisine and Jiaodong cuisine, Shandong cuisine, clean, pure and not greasy, is characterized by its emphasis on aroma, freshness, crispness and tenderness.
3) Characterized by its spicy and pungent flavors, Sichuan cuisine, with a myriad of tastes, emphasizes the use of chili and Pepper powder.
4) Steaming and stir-frying are most frequently used to preserve the ingredients' natural flavors.
5) It is renowned not only for its material selection but for the fine workmanship in cutting, matching, cooking, and arranging.

2. Translate the following sentences into English.
1) 一般说来中国菜可分为八大地方菜。
2) 山东菜常用大葱和大蒜作调料。
3) 四川菜中,食用草药、家禽、鸟常用作做菜的原料。
4) 淮阳菜的风味是清淡、鲜嫩、味甜,而且菜式精美雅致。
5) 安徽菜常加入火腿提味,加入冰糖提鲜。

IV. **Complete the following dialogues.**

1. A: _____ (您点菜吗)?
   B: What do you recommend we order?

A: ＿＿＿＿＿＿＿＿＿＿＿＿＿＿＿＿（我们的特色菜有）Sweet and Sour Pork(古老肉), Fish-flavored Diced Chicken(鱼香鸡丁), Deep-fried Fish Rolls(炸鱼卷), Stir-fried Beancurd with Crab Meat(蟹肉豆腐).

B: I think they are worth to trying. Let me look at the menu.

2. A: ＿＿＿＿＿＿＿＿＿＿＿＿＿＿＿＿＿＿＿？（牛排您要几分熟，熟透的、中等的，还是嫩一点？）

B: ＿＿＿＿＿＿＿＿＿＿＿＿＿＿＿．（我要熟透的）

3. A: Good morning, sir. Can I help you?

B: ＿＿＿＿＿＿＿＿＿＿＿＿＿＿．（我要定一张两人桌，今晚用。）

A: ＿＿＿＿＿＿＿＿＿＿＿＿＿＿？（我们什么时间恭候您？）

B: About 6:00.

V. Build up your vocabulary.

1. Fill in the blanks with the words or expressions given below. Change their forms where necessary

flavor; technique; aroma; edible; originate from; divide into; consist of; be characterized by

1) There are many ＿＿＿＿ mushrooms on the mountain behind the village.
2) She admired the pianist's perfect ＿＿＿＿.
3) The students can ＿＿＿＿ three groups.
4) This club ＿＿＿＿ more than 100 members.
5) That shop sells ice cream in 20 different ＿＿＿＿.
6) Coffee gives out an ＿＿＿＿.
7) The camel ＿＿＿＿ the ability to go for long periods without water.
8) The new style of dancing ＿＿＿＿ the island.

2. Match the following two columns.

A. 麻辣牛肉　　　　　a. Sugar-coated Fruits
B. 干煸牛肉丝　　　　b. Meat-filled Buns in Small Steamer
C. 冰糖葫芦　　　　　c. Shrimp Stir-fried Rice
D. 酸辣汤　　　　　　d. Hot and Peppery Beef
E. 拔丝香蕉　　　　　e. Braised Pork in Brown Sauce
F. 小笼包子　　　　　f. Dry-fried Beef Shreds
G. 红烧肉　　　　　　g. Hot and Sour Soup
H. 草莓圣代　　　　　h. Hot Candied Banana
I. 虾仁炒饭　　　　　i. Spaghetti with tomato sauce
J. 茄汁意大利面条　　j. Strawberry Sundae

VI. Make up a dialogue according to the given situation.

Some foreigners come to the restaurant to have a dinner. A waitress is asked to introduce Chinese food. She tells them the features of some famous regional cuisines and the specialties in the restaurant.

VII. Mini Dialogues.

W = Waitress   G = Guest

Dialogue A

W: Good evening. Do you have any reservation?

G: Yes. We have a reservation for a table for four at 6 o'clock under the name of Mr Green.

W: Just a moment, please. I'll take a look at our reservation book. Yes, Mr Green, a table for four, 6 o'clock. This way, please.

G: Thank you.

Dialogue B

G: Waitress, we'll take the bill now.

W: Yes, sir. Just a moment, please... Here it is, sir. It amounts to two hundred and forty-eight yuan. Please have a check on it.

G: Let me have a look at it. Mm, all right. Here is three hundred yuan.

W: I'll go to the cashier's counter to settle the bill for you. Wait a moment, please... Here is the invoice and change, fifty-two yuan. Thank you for coming. Goodbye.

G: Goodbye.

VIII. Practical Writing.

Menu 菜单

Sample 1

```
                        COLD DISHES
Shredded Chicken with Peanuts & Chilli  ············  ￥18
Sichuan Drunken Chicken  ·························  ￥20
Sliced Pork with Garlic  ···························  ￥15
Ham and Sausage  ································  ￥15
Fresh Prawn Salad  ······························  ￥35
Lobster Salad with Fruits  ·························  ￥38
```

Sample 2

Desserts List	
CHEESECAKE ··	$4.29
Rich, smooth and creamy cheesecake over strawberry sauce	
MOLTEN CHOCOLATE CAKE ·································	$4.29
Warm chocolate cake with chocolate fudge filling. Topped with vanilla ice cream under a crunchy chocolate shell.	
CHOCOLATE CHIP PARADISE PIE ·························	$4.79
We start with a warm, chewy bar layered with chocolate chips, walnuts and coconut. Topped with vanilla ice cream and drizzled with hot fudge and caramel.	
FROSTY CHOCOLATE SHAKE ·······························	$2.99
Creamy & delicious. Thick & frosty chocolate shake with chocolate sprinkles.	

Write a menu according to the given information.

某酒店为某公司举办一次招待宴会,有外宾参加,请为其设计一份宴会菜单。

Text B Different Table Manners between Chinese and Westerners

In China today we have many chances of having a dinner in a Western restaurant or eating with foreigners. Therefore, it is helpful for us to know some rules about Western table manners, for they are completely different from what we usually do.

In most Western restaurants and homes, dinner is enjoyed with hushed voices. And it is bad manner to speak with one's mouth full of food, so speaking only occurs before one takes in food or after he or she swallow it. On the contrary, Chinese people can have conversation when having meals. The dinning table is a forum for talking about business, education, and other worthy topics. But the same rule that both Chinese and Western people must follow is that the gloomy matters such as death, accident, and other misfortunes shouldn't be mentioned. Especially, according to Western manners, if one have to use the toilet, the proper way is to avoid mentioning what it is that he or she is going to do and one would say, "May I be excused, please? I need to wash my hands."

In the West, eating must be done as quietly as possible. No eating noises are allowed. Therefore, one should eat with mouth closed. "Slurping" soup, coffee, or wine is also forbidden. If any sound is created by one's intake of food or beverage, it is considered as a bad manner. This rule is shared by Chinese people.

Knife is used only for cutting. In North America, the fork is held in the left hand and the knife in the right hand while food is being cut, and then the knife is put down and the fork is transferred to the right hand for eating. In Europe, the fork is kept in the left hand and knife in the right all the time. However, food should not be cut into small pieces before one eats it. The proper way is to cut one small piece at a time, and then eat it.

In Western manners, one should sit at the table in an upright position with the recessive hand in the lap holding the napkin, while the dominant hand holds the fork or spoon. The only time the both hands are allowed to be put on the table is when one is using a knife to cut food, but as soon as the cut-ting is done, the recessive hand goes back to the lap. Also, elbows are not allowed on the table. One should not try to take any food across the table but ask for it when there is a pause in the conversation, "Would you please pass the sugar?"

In China, however, chopsticks are the main tool for eating. They are made either from wood, bamboo or from plastic and held in the right hand. It is ill-mannered to play chopsticks during meals. Besides, it is a taboo to stick the chopsticks in the rice bowl upright, for it is the way only appearing on the funeral or memorial ceremony in China. In Chinese manners, both hands are used for eating with the left holding the bowl and the right holding the chopsticks. And it is widly accepted that when one offers other people food to show his or her friendship and politeness, it is a good manner to use public chopsticks.

For many Westerners, the Chinese dinner table is rather strange, for there are no forks or knives for the Westerners to use. And the lively atmosphere may leave them at a loss for what to do though it seems fantastic. So it is better to explain some Chinese table manners to the westerners before dinner.

Notes

1. The dinning table is a forum for talking about business, education, and other worthy topics.
   饭桌是公开讨论生意、教育和其他有价值的话题的地方。
2. "Slurping" soup, coffee, or wine is also forbidden.
   咕嘟咕嘟地喝汤、咖啡或酒也是不允许的。
3. In Western manners, one should sit at the table in an upright position with the

recessive hand in the lap holding the napkin, while the dominant hand holds the fork or spoon.

西方人的餐桌礼仪是在桌前身体要坐直，不拿餐具的手放在腿上拿住餐巾，而主要用的那只手拿着叉或勺。

4. It is a taboo to stick the chopsticks in the rice bowl upright, for it is the way only appearing on the funeral or memorial ceremony in China.

把筷子竖着插在饭碗里是一种禁忌，因为在中国，只有在葬礼或纪念仪式上才这样做。

5. It is widly accepted that when one offers other people food to show his or her friendship and politeness, it is a good manner to use public chopsticks. 人们普遍认为，当给别人夹取食物以示友好和礼貌时，好的礼仪是用公用筷子。

Exercises: Mark the following statements with "T" (Ture) or "F" (False) according to Text B.

1. According to western manners, eating must be done as quietly as possible.
2. In China, people can slurp soup, coffee, or wine.
3. Chinese people can have conversation when having meals.
4. In North America, the fork is kept in the left hand and knife in the right all the time.
5. In Western manners, people can take food across the table.
6. Both Chinese people and Western people avoid mentioning gloomy matters when having meals.
7. In Western restaurants, one can cut food into small pieces before eating it.
8. In China, it is a good manner to use public chopsticks to offer other people food.

Text C How to Cook Mapo Beancurd

It is said that Chenmapo beancurd can be traced back to the nineteenth century. This dish gained its name simply due to the fact that the beancurd was first cooked in a special way by a grandmother with many pockmarks on her face, who was called "mapo" in Chengdu dialect. Now Mapo beancurd has a world-wide reputation.

The popularity of Mapo beancurd comes from its well-known taste of the tender beancurd cooked in a special way.

The ingredients should be prepared first, including: 500 g beancurd, cut into small cubes, blanched; 150 g lean pork, finely minced; 3 garlic sprouts, chopped into segments; rapeseed oil; 1 tablespoon of fermented black beans, chopped; 2 pickled red chilies, chopped; 2 tablespoons of soy sauce; 1 ~ 2 teaspoons of Pixian bean paste; a half teaspoon of salt; 2 teaspoons of sugar; a half teaspoon of Sichuan peppercorns, ground; a cup (250 ml) of chicken stock; 1 tablespoon of cornstarch, mixed with a little cold water.

Next, heat the oil in a wok, and stir-fry the pork and garlic sprouts until they are half cooked. Then add the black beans, chillies, soy sauce and Pixian bean paste and stir-fry together for about 1 ~ 2 minutes. And then add other seasoning ingredients, except the cornstarch. When the mixture is boiled, slide in the beancurd cubes and simmer for about 2 minutes. Finally, add the stirred mixture of cornstarch. Carefully stir until it is thickened. The delicious and nutritious Mapo beancurd is ready.

Notes

1. pockmark 痘痕，麻点
2. blanched 焯过的，用热水烫的
3. lean 精瘦的
4. minced 切碎的
5. garlic sprouts 蒜苗
6. chopped into segments 剁成段
7. soy sauce 酱油
8. Pixian bean paste 郫县豆瓣酱
9. peppercorn 花椒籽
10. ground 捣碎的
11. chicken stock 鸡汤原汁
12. wok 锅
13. cornstarch 玉米淀粉

Exercises: Fill in the blanks according to Text C.

Cut the beancurd into small _____, and _____ in boiling water to get rid of its odd smell. Ladle out and set aside. Very finely _____ the lean pork, and _____ garlic sprouts into _____. Heat the oil in a wok, and _____ the pork and garlic sprouts until half cooked. Add the black beans, chillies, soy sauce and Pixian bean paste and _____ together for about 1 ~ 2 minutes, and then add the remaining seasoning ingredients, _____ the cornstarch, and bring to the boil. _____ in the beancurd and _____ for about 2 minutes. Carefully stir in the cornstarch mixed with a little cold water, simmering gerntly until _____.

Unit 8　Chinese Tea

Study structure
Text A (**Intensive Reading**): **Chinese Tea**
Dialogues
New Words and Expressions
Exercises
Text B (**Extensive Reading**): **Public Houses**
Text C (**Supplementary Reading**): **Tibetan Buttered Tea and Mongolian Milk Tea**

Summary of the Text

　　This unit deals with five types of Chinese Tea and benefit of tea-drinking in Text A, the main features of pubs in Britain and some rules of ordering drinks in pubs in Text B, and the main features and process of making Tibetan buttered tea and Mongolian milk tea in Text C.

Text A　Chinese Tea

　　China is the homeland of tea. Tea growing in China can be traced back to the period of the Warring States. And more than a thousand years ago, China tea as an export began to be known all over the world. It is believed that the word for tea derives from the Chinese character "茶" (cha). The English word "tea" sounds similar to the pronunciation of "茶" in Xiamen dialect (Amoy) although it sounds different from the pronunciation of "cha" in standard Chinese.

Types of Chinese Tea

　　According to the different ways in which it is processed, Chinese tea can be classified into five types: green tea, black tea, Wulong tea, compressed tea (brick tea), and jasmine tea.

　　Green tea is the one which keeps the original colour of the tea leaves without fermentation during processing. It consists mainly of Longjing of Zhejiang Province, Maofeng of Huangshan Mountain in Anhui Province and Biluochun produced in

Jiangsu.

Black tea, known as "red tea" (hong cha) in China, needs fermentation before baking. The best brands of black tea are Qihong of Anhui, Dianhong of Yunnan, Suhong of Jiangsu, Chuanhong of Sichuan and Xianghong of Hunan.

Wulong tea is processed half way between the green and the black teas, being made after partial fermentation. It is a specialty from the provinces on China's southeast coast—Fujian, Guangdong and Taiwan.

Compressed tea is good for transport and storage and is mainly supplied to the remote area. Most of the compressed tea is in the form of bricks; it is, therefore, generally called "brick tea", though it is sometimes also in the form of cakes and bowls. It is mainly produced in Hubei, Hunan, Sichuan and Yunnan.

Jasmine tea is made by mixing dried tea leaves and jasmine flowers. It is a well-known favorite with the northerners of China and with a growing number of foreigners.

Benefit of Tea-Drinking

Chinese people like to have a cup of tea after meal, and they usually offer tea when visitors call. Tea has been one of the daily necessities in China.

Moreover, drinking tea can help people keep fit. Tea may help resolve fat and promote digestion. It is, therefore, of special importance to people who live mainly on meat, like many of the national minorities in China. A popular proverb among them says, "Rather live without salt for three days than without tea for a single day."

Tea is also rich in various vitamins. And for smokers, it helps to discharge nicotine out of the system. For drunken people, it is said that tea can help them sober up.

However, it does not mean that the stronger the tea, the more advantages it will yield. It is reported that constant drinking of over-strong tea may result in heart and blood-pressure disorders in some people, and put a brown color on the teeth of young people.

Finally, it is important to remember that the boiling water mustn't be used for tea-making, for it will destroy vitamins in the tea leaves. The most suitable tempreture is lower than 80 ℃.

New Words and Expressions

trace	/treis/	v. 追溯,追踪
		n. 痕迹,形迹,足迹
derive	/di'raiv/	v. 起源(于……)
Amoy	/ə'mɔi/	n. 厦门方言
classify	/'klæsifai/	v. 把……分类
compress	/kəm'pres/	v. 压缩,紧压
jasmine	/'dʒæsmin/	n. 茉莉
fermentation	/ˌfəːmen'teiʃən/	n. 发酵
partial	/'paːʃl/	adj. 部分的,局部的,不完全的
favorite	/'feivərit/	adj. 心爱的,最喜爱的
		n. 心爱的人或物,最喜爱的东西
necessity	/ni'sesəti/	n. 必要的东西,必需品
resolve	/ri'zɔlv/	v. 分解;下决心,决定;解决
digestion	/di'dʒestʃən/	n. 消化,消化作用
minority	/mai'nɔrəti/	n. 少数,少数派,少数民族
proverb	/'prɔvɜːb/	n. 谚语,格言
vitamin	/'vitəmin/	n. 维生素,维他命
discharge	/dis'tʃaːdʒ/	v. 排放,排出,流出;释放,解雇
nicotine	/'nikətiːn/	n. 尼古丁
sober	/'səubə/	v. 变冷静,变严肃
		adj. 清醒的,没喝醉的,冷静的,严肃的
yield	/jiːld/	v. 带来利益,生产;屈服
trace (back) to		追溯
derive from		起源于
keep fit		保持健康
rather (...) than		宁可……而不;与其说……不如说
rich in		富于;盛产
sober up		酒醒
result in		导致,引起

Notes

1. green tea 绿茶
2. black tea 红茶

3. Wulong tea 乌龙茶
4. compressed tea/ brick tea 砖茶
5. jasmine tea 茉莉花茶
6. Longjing 龙井茶
7. Maofeng 毛峰茶
8. Biluochun 碧螺春
9. Qihong 祁(门)红茶
10. Dianhong 滇红茶
11. Suhong 苏红茶
12. Chuanhong 川红茶
13. Xianghong 湘红茶
14. Rather live without salt for three days than without tea for a single day.
    宁可三日无盐,不可一日无茶。

Dialogues

Dialogue A: In the Bar

W = Waiter   J = Jack   S = Susan

W: Good evening! Would you like something to drink?

J: Yes, but give us some minutes to look through the drink list first.

W: OK.

J: Let's see... cocktail, Brandies, Sherry, Liqueur, Scotch... Here is beer. I'll have Five Star. What about you, Susan?

S: I'll have a Sangria.

J: What is a Sangria?

S: It is a cocktail consists of red wine, lemon juice, orange juice and sugar.

J: That sounds good. OK, waiter, one Five Star for me and one Sangria for her.

W: One Five Star and one Sangria. Thank you.

Dialogue B: Complaining About a Late Order

W: Waitress   G: Guest   W: Wine waiter

G: Waitress, what happened to my order of drinks? We've waited for 20 minutes, but they still haven't arrived.

W: I'm sorry, sir. I'll see the wine waiter for you.

G: Well, please hurry up. We can't wait much longer.

W: I'll be with you in a moment.

……

W: I'm sorry to have kept you waiting. Your order is coming, sir.

G: All right.

Ww: Here is your order. I'm so sorry for the delay, sir. Please enjoy your drinks.

Notes

1. cocktail 鸡尾酒
2. Brandy 白兰地
3. Sherry 雪利酒
4. Liqueur 利口酒
5. Scotch 苏格兰威士忌
6. Five Star 五星啤酒
7. Sangria 香格里

Useful Expressions and Patterns

1. Would you like something to drink?
   您想喝点什么吗?
2. What would you like to drink?
   您想喝点什么?
3. What can I make for you today?
   今天给您来点什么?
4. What would you like to have today?
   今天您来点什么?
5. What is it going to be tonight?
   今晚来杯什么?
6. What will it be today?
   今天来点什么?
7. Give us some minutes to look through the drink list first.
   给我们几分钟先看看饮料单。
8. I'd like to see the menu.
   让我看看菜单。
9. What happened to my order of drinks?
   我点的饮料呢? 怎么回事?
10. We can't wait much longer.
    我们不能再等下去了。

11. I'm sorry to have kept you waiting.
    对不起,让您久等了。
12. I'm so sorry for the delay.
    实在抱歉,(饮料)上晚了,耽搁了您的时间。
13. Please enjoy your drinks.
    请用您的饮料。

Exercises

I. Answer the following questions according to Text A.

1. How many types of tea are there in China? What are they?
2. What is the difference between black tea and green tea?
3. Can you tell any famous brands of green tea?
4. What are the features of compressed tea?
5. What is the benefit of tea-drinking?

II. Mark the following statements with "T"(True) or "F"(False) according to Text A.

1. Jasmine tea is a well-known favorite with the southerners of China.
2. Tea helps resolve fat and promote digestion.
3. Tea can help drunken people sober up.
4. The stronger the tea, the more advantages it will yield.
5. We must use boiling water to make tea.

III. Translation.

1. Translate the following sentences into Chinese.
1) The English word "tea" sounds similar to the pronunciation of "茶" in Xiamen dialect(Amoy) although it sounds different from the pronunciation of "cha" in standard Chinese.
2) According to the different ways in which it is processed, Chinese tea can be classified into five types: green tea, black tea, Wulong tea, compressed tea (brick tea), and jasmine tea.
3) Wulong tea is processed half way between the green and the black teas, being made after partial fermentation.
4) Most of the compressed tea is in the form of bricks; it is, therefore, generally called "brick tea", though it is sometimes also in the form of cakes and bowls.
5) It is reported that constant drinking of over-strong tea may result in heart and

blood-pressure disorders in some people, and put a brown color on the teeth of young people.

2. Translate the following sentences into English.
1) 中国人种茶的历史可以追溯到 2 000 多年以前。
2) 砖茶易于运输和贮存,主要供往偏远地区。
3) 茉莉花茶是北方人最喜爱喝的茶。
4) 以肉食为主的少数民族经常饮茶来促进消化。
5) 我与其说是疲惫不如说是厌倦。

IV. Complete the following dialogue.

W = Waiter   G = Guest

1. W: Good evening! _____ (您想喝点什么)?
   G: _____ (我要一杯鸡尾酒).
   W: We have Manhattan, White Lady, Stinger, Negroni, Margarita. _____ (您要哪一种)?
   G: Give me a Margarita.

2. W: Room service. _____ (您有什么事吗)?
   G: I'm Albert Dodge in 815. _____ (我的早餐怎么回事)? I ordered it half an hour ago and it hasn't come yet.
   W: _____ (我很抱歉耽误您时间了). Hang on a minute, please. I'll check your order with the chef...
   W: Thank you for waiting, sir. Your order is ready now and we will send it up immediately. _____ (您再稍等一下好吗)?
   G: All right.

V. Vocabulary and Structure.

1. Fill in the blanks with the expressions given below. Change their forms where necessary.

trace back to; keep fit; sober up; result in; rich in; derive from; rater than; the more... the more

1) A lot of English words _____ Latin.
2) His fear of water can _____ to his childhood experience.
3) Exercise _____ people _____.
4) I think he, _____ you, is to blame.
5) This area is very _____ cotton.
6) Put him to bed until he _____.
7) _____ you know, _____ you will realize how little you know.

8) His careless speech _____ much argument.
2. Fill in the blanks with the words given below. Change their forms where necessary.

| compress; favorite; minority; resolve; discharge; classify; yield; necessity |

1) Many libraries _____ books by subject or author.
2) He _____ his clothes into a bag.
3) That singer is one of her _____.
4) Food, clothing, and shelter are _____ in our daily life.
5) He _____ that nothing should hold him back.
6) Only a _____ of students receive the scholarship.
7) He _____ for dishonesty.
8) We'll never _____ to force.
3. Match the following two columns.
A. 四川   a. Longjing
B. 云南   b. Maofeng
C. 湖南   c. Bilouchun
D. 浙江   e. Qihong
E. 安徽   f. Dianhong
F. 江苏   g. Xianghong
                  h. Suhong

VI. Make up a dialogue according to the given situation.

A guest asks for room service. There isn't any more wine in his mini-bar. He asks more drinks. Don't forget the guest's name and the room number.

VII. Mini dialogues.

W = Waiter   G = Guest

Dialogue A

W: Can I get you something to drink?
G: Let me have a look at the drink list.
W: Here it is.
G: I'd like to start with a cocktail. What is a Tom Collins?
W: It is made from gin, soda water, lemon juice and sugar.
G: It sounds good. Give me a Tom Collins.

Dialogue B

W: Room service. May I help you?
G: Can you send up some drinks?

W: What would you like, madam?

G: Two whiskies on the rocks(两瓶威士忌加冰), one rum(郎姆酒) and an orange soft drink.

W: Your name and room number, please?

G: Janet Lee. I'm in 622.

W: Anything else?

G: No, thank you.

VIII. Practical Writing.

Formal invitation

Sample 1

> Mr. and Mrs. Wang Mingyuan
> Request the pleasure of the company of
> Mr. and Mrs. Donald White
> To welcom Mr. and Mrs. Ralph Jackson
> At Mudan Hall, Gloria Hotel,
> On Friday, 10th May at 7:00 p.m.
>
> R.S.V.P.
> 67854655

Sample 2

> You are cordially invited by
> The President of Red Star Company Mr. Wang Xin
> To attend an Anniversary Reception
> From 11:30 a.m. to 13:30 p.m. on Monday, May 9, 2005
> At Lijiang Restaurant
>
> R.S.V.P.
> 7668523

Write a formal invitation for your boss to a foreign business partner asking him or her to dinner.

Text B Public Houses

A public house, usually known as a pub, is a drinking establishment found mainly in Britain, Ireland, Australia, New Zealand and other countries influenced by an English cultural heritage. There are approximately 60,000 public houses in the United Kingdom. They are culturally, socially and traditionally different from places such as cafes or bars found elsewhere in the world.

In general, pubs are open from 11 am to 11 pm, but times may vary with each establishment. They offer a wide and varied selection of brews, perhaps as many as 20 different types of ales, lagers, stouts and bitters. Most are draft, some in bottles and a few in cans. Most pubs also serve wine and hard liquor. They will also have non-alcoholic drinks, coke, orange juice tea and coffee, but not a large range.

Most pubs offer people a cheerful and pleasant place to sit and relax with friends, have a reasonably priced meal, read a book or paper, or play a game. A number of traditional games were often played in pubs including darts, billiards, and skittles etc. In recent years the game of pool is very popular in British pub culture. In addition, many pubs now provide video games or pop music, or show football games on big screen televisions.

In addition, there are some distinctive rules of which foreign travelers are expected to be aware when they visit a pub in Britain.

There is no waiter service in the pub. You have to go to the bar to order your drinks and food. But if you are in a large group, it is better to have one person go up to the bar to make orders and pay for the drinks.

There is no orderly queue at the bar though there are usually many people there. But the barman knows the exact order, so you needn't worry that someone would jump the queue. What you should do to let him know you are waiting to be served is to catch the barman's eye instead of making any noise or too much gesticulation. Don't shout out, snap your fingers or wave money about. You can hold an empty glass or money in your hand but do not wave it around. You can also have a slightly anxious, hopeful or expectant expression to show your eagerness.

It's important to say "please" and "thank you" to show your politeness.

Don't tip the barman. The custom is to buy him a drink. For a tip would indicate a service role for the barman. But buying him a drink is to show your friendship. But instead of saying "Can I buy you a drink?", the proper way is to say "and will you have one yourself?" or "and one for yourself?" They may not drink it at once but may have one later when they are not so busy. If you are still there, they will usually catch your eye and raise their glass as a sign of thanks.

Notes

1. establishment 设施
2. ale 淡色啤酒(色淡而味香及酒精成分较浓的啤酒)
3. lager 淡啤酒(低温杀菌后适于贮藏的啤酒)
4. stout 黑啤酒
5. bitter 苦啤酒
6. draft (由木桶装的酒中)汲出, 抽出   eg. draft beer 生啤酒
7. darts 飞镖游戏
8. billiards 台球
9. skittles 九柱戏
10. pool 赌博, 赌注
11. gesticulation 示意的动作
12. snap your fingers 打响指

Exercises: Answer the following questions accordiy to Text B.

1. What types of drinks are offered in pubs?
2. What are the traditional games played in pubs?
3. Is there waiter service in Britain pubs?
4. Is there orderly queue at the bar?
5. How can you let the barman know you are waiting to be served?
6. Is it polite to tip the barman?

Text C   Tibetan Buttered Tea and Mongolian Milk Tea

The Tibetans like drinking buttered tea, the most common tea in Tibet. According to historical records, Princess Wencheng in Tang Dynasty introduced tea to Tibet, and spread the habit of drinking tea, but we don't know when the Tibetans invented buttered tea. Today, however, they make and drink buttered tea every day.

There is an unique way to making buttered tea. The Tibetan people prefer their tea thick and strong, so they usually use brick tea. First, tea leaves are boiled in the kettle, which is usually made of silver, copper, aluminum, or other metals and which is usually decorated with gold or silver designs. Second, the brew is strained into a barrel. And then some materials and butter are added. The most common materials are chestnut paste, sesame powder, peanuts, melon seed kernels, pine nuts, eggs and salt. The materials are stirred before being put into the kettle. Finally, the mixture is warmed on the fire for about one minute instead of being boiled. The buttered tea will then be ready.

When guests visit a Tibetan family, a special ritual must be followed in drinking buttered tea. The hostess first offers Tibetan traditional food, Zanba (a dough of roasted Qingke barley flour and tea) in a bamboo box, and then a set of brilliant teacups, which are made of porcelain or wood and usually inlaid with silver or copper, are put in front of each person. After that, the host will pour the buttered tea into each cup and say warmly, "Please drink the tea!" The guest will drink the tea and eat Zanba with fingers. The buttered tea, a little salty, is rich, fragrant and delicious. But the cup should not be emptied. Some tea should be left, which will indicate that the guest appreciates the host's skill in making the tea and desires more. The host will then refill the cup. After the third cup, if the guest has had enough, the cup can be drained and the dregs thrown on the ground. The host will not refill the cup.

Mongolians never have meals without milk tea. They drink "three teas" everyday. It is said that the Mongolian milk tea may be influenced by Tibetan buttered tea. But it has some distinct qualities.

Mongolian milk tea is not accompanied by Zanba, but by some Mongolian snacks, such as fried rice, milk cakes, deep fried milk products and boiled mutton.

There is also a special way to make tea with milk. First, brick tea is pounded into pieces, which are put into an iron wok or an aluminum or copper kettle. Next, water is added and then boiled for about 10 minutes. When the water turns reddish-brown, milk and salt are added and stirred. Thus the hot, fragrant and delicious tea will be ready. If the tea is boiled in a wok, it must be strained into a kettle and kept warm on a slow fire so that people may drink it any time.

The Mongolian people usually make a kettle of tea after they get up in the morning and keep it warm on a slow fire all day. Generally, a kettle of tea is better to boil once, but lesser well-off families might add a few tea leaves and boil it a second and third time.

Notes

1. Tibetan Buttered Tea 西藏酥油茶
2. Mongolian Milk Tea 蒙古奶茶
3. brew 酿造物
4. chestnut paste 栗子糊
5. sesame powder 芝麻粉
6. peanuts 花生
7. melon seed kernels 西瓜籽仁
8. pine nuts 松子
9. ritual 仪式，惯例
10. Zanba 糌粑
11. barley 大麦
12. dregs（沉在饮料底部剩余的）残渣，渣滓

Exercises: Answer the following questions according to Text C.

1. When was tea introduced to Tibet?
2. What kind of tea is usually used to make Tibetan buttered tea?
3. What are the most common materials added to the buttered tea?
4. What is Zanba?
5. How should the guests make the host know they have drinked enough tea?
6. What can people eat with Mongolian milk tea?

Unit 9　Sightseeing

Study structure
Text A (Intensive Reading): Reasons for People to Travel
Dialogues
New Words and Expressions
Exercises
Text B (Extensive Reading): The Travel Agency
Text C (Supplementary Reading): Thomas Cook

Summary of the Text

  Nowadays, in order to satisfy the needs and curiosity of themselves, train the body and improve their knowledge, people will choose tourism. The growth of tourism has become a contemporary phenomenon because many reasons, such as much more leisure time, discretionary income and the improvement in transportation encourage people to travel. So the travel agency is very necessary. In the history of the travel industry, Thomas Cook is a name of significance.

Text A　Reasons for People to Travel

  The growth of tourism has become a contemporary phenomenon experienced by all countries in the world. International tourist arrivals alone reached as high as 546 million in 1994 and is forecasted to rise to 937 million in 2010, according to WTO. But why do people travel so much?

  According to Maslow, there is a hierarchy of universal wants and needs found in every human being. At the lower levels of the hierarchy are the needs for survival. At the top of the hierarchy there are the needs for self-actualization of self-realization, that is, the need to develop one's own potential, the need for aesthetic stimulation, the need to create or to build one's own personality and character, etc. After one's own survival is well established, people will naturally seek the gratification of other needs. Then tourism turns out to be a good solution, since it provides ample chances to satisfy most of the needs, and the needs, in turn, constitute major motivational factors for people to travel and go on vacation.

Probably the most common reason for travel is associated with our physical well-being. Actually, travel for sports is one of the fastest growing generators of travel. The motivational force of spectator sports is, however, more complex. There is the desire to get away from routine, to identify with teams and individuals, which gives people a sense of belonging, and to dream of the role one would fulfill if he were playing. Here, the effect may be felt more mentally than physically. In the fast-moving modern society where strain and stress have become part of an individual's life, people tend to have a change in environment and activities in order to rest and relax.

Another important motivator is connected with culture and curiosity, which is expressed by the desire to know about other places of countries, and to search for all kinds of experiences. No one seems to doubt that travel broadens the mind. It was the desire for knowledge that was the reason for the growth of the Grand Tour. Today this desire is widely encouraged by modern mass media and communications such as television and airplane, which find their ways into every corner of the world. After one has traveled to a particular place, he tends to be more interested in news items or television programs about it. By learning about other cultures one can also discover his own, and thus truly enriches his mind.

The need for belonging is manifested in the desire to visit friends or relatives, to meet new people and make new friendships. People, by and large are social beings, who want communication and contact with others. In travel, people with this intention usually put more emphasis on the route of the trip than on the destination. Of course, it does help to encourage travel if the friend or relative lives in an exotic or interesting place. To cater to this need, many travel agencies specialize in certain ethnic areas and people, providing specialized tours to return and visit "the old country" where some tourists may pick up a genealogical line or find their roots.

When people travel to a conference to increase their professional knowledge, they are concerned with their own personal development. Their self-esteem is enhanced. People also seek esteem from others. It is said that in tourism "mass follows class". The implication is that there are places that special people go, and some go to be like those special people. To be the first to go to an exotic place, or to go where certain types of people go, offers some excitement and creates an illusion of enviable sophistication among one's friends.

A combination of needs and desires has given impetus to one of the largest industries today—the travel industry. Nevertheless, people need more than motivations in order to travel. Two other elements are essential before one will seriously consider planning a trip: they are leisure and discretionary income.

Leisure can be defined as freedom from the necessity to labor. Two aspects of leisure were and are important in promoting tourism: the time available for leisure, and peoples' attitude toward leisure. Since World War Two, the amount of leisure available to an individual has, in general, increased. The workweek has decreased from sixty hours to forty hours per week, and the reduction of the workweek will still continue in most developed countries as well as some developing countries. In addition, changing social conditions have introduced and established leisure time as a way of life, and leisure became a justifiable aspect of the society. The increased time available began to be spent in the pursuit of recreation and pleasurable activities other than work.

Discretionary income, or disposable income, is money not needed for personal essentials such as food, clothing, health-care, transportation, and so forth. Smaller family size and an increase of women in the labor market have made today's family more affluent, which greatly promotes the tourist industry.

The improvement in transportation has facilitated travel on a large scale. The explosion of railway and automobile travel was followed by dynamic improvements in air service. Today, in many countries, elaborate road systems have been built so that a person can go from border to border or even across national borders in the case of Europe without being affected by a single red light or two-way traffic on the same roadway. The vast network of roads and air connections and the mass production of the car at a price many people can afford have led to the development of a tourist industry unmatched in history. With increasing affluence and leisure, and a relative decrease in cost of travel, the growth of the travel industry will surely continue.

Dialogues

Dialogue A

A: Good morning, madam.
B: Good morning. Today I can offer the whole day for sightseeing. Can you make a suggestion where to go?
A: Sure. How about going to the Bund in the morning? You can see it alive with a lot of people doing morning exercises, fan dance, Chinese boxing and so on.
B: That must be very exciting.

A: Exactly. Then visit the Yu Garden, which is within easy reach. It's one of the most famous scenic spots in Shanghai. It's worth visiting. By the way, you can have a taste of typical Chinese tea in the teahouse there.

B: That's a good idea.

A: In the afternoon, you'd better cross the Huangpu River—the mother river of Shanghai—to have a bird's-eye view of Shanghai at the top floor of Shanghai Oriental Pearl TV Tower, which is the highest TV tower in Asia.

B: Great.

Dialogue B

A: This is my first travel to England, and would you give me some suggestion?

B: Will you stay here long?

A: Only five days on business.

B: There are many tourist attractions. You should really visit Great Park. Have you been here yet?

A: No, I am going there tomorrow.

B: I have some information about them. Would you like to have a look?

A: It is very kind of you.

B: Here you are.

New Words and Expressions

1. phenomenon /fi'nɔminən/ n. 现象
2. hierarchy /'haiəra:ki/ n. 现实,现实化
3. ultimately /'ʌltimitli/ adv. 最终地,极限地
4. actualization /ˌæktʃuəlaiˈzeiʃn/ n. 现实,现实化
5. aesthetic /i:s'θetik/ adj. 美的,艺术的
6. ample /'æmpl/ adj. 足够的
7. motivational /ˌməutiˈveiʃənl/ adj. 动力的,有动机的
8. individual /ˌindiˈvidjuəl/ n. 个人
9. curiosity /ˌkjuəriˈɔsiti/ n. 好奇心
10. manifest /'mænifest/ v. 证明,显示
11. ethnic /'eθnik/ adj. 种族的,人种学的
12. exotic /igˈzɔtik/ adj. 外国的,奇异的
13. genealogical /ˌdʒi:niəˈlɔdʒikəl/ adj. 家谱的,家系的
14. esteem /isˈti:m/ n. 尊重,尊敬
15. implication /ˌimpliˈkeiʃən/ n. 含义,暗示

16.	illusion	/i'lju:ʒən/	n. 幻觉,幻影
17.	enviable	/'enviəbl/	adj. 值得羡慕的
18.	justifiable	/'dʒʌstifaiəbl/	adj. 正当的,有理的
19.	affluent	/'æfluənt/	adj. 富裕的,丰富的
20.	facilitate	/fə'siliteit/	v. 便利,促进
21.	dynamic	/dai'næmik/	adj. 有力的,有生气的
22.	affluence	/'æfluəns/	n. 丰富,富裕

Notes

1. self-actualization 自我实现
2. Maslow 马斯洛(Albraham Harold Maslow, 1908~1970) 美国心理学家,人本主义心理学的主要创始人之一。
3. Probably the most common reason for travel is associated with our physical well-being.
   或许,旅游最常见的理由是和我们的身体健康有关的。
4. In the fast-moving modern society where strain and stress have been become part of an individual's life...
   在迅速发展的现代社会中,紧张和压力已成为个人生活的一部分……
   where 引出定语从句,修饰名词 society, 此处 where 的意思为 in/at which。
5. It was the desire for knowledge that was the reason for the growth of the Grand Tour.
   大旅游的原因正是由求知欲引起的。
   the Grand Tour 是指旧时英国贵族学生赴欧洲大陆作为最终学程的大旅游。
6. By learning about other culture, one can also discover his own, and thus truly enriches his mind.
   通过了解其他文化,一个人也能发展自身的文化,从而真正丰富自己的思想。
   by 引起的介词短语作状语,意思为"通过……方法",如:
   Only by doing so can we strengthen our ties with the masses.
   只有这样做,我们才能加强和群众的联系。
7. The other elements are essential before one will seriously consider planning a trip...
   在一个人认真考虑制定旅游计划之前,另外两个基本要素是要考虑……
   动词 consider 后跟动名词作宾语,而不能用不定式。

8. Smaller family sizes and an increase of woman in the labor market have made today's family more affluent, which greatly promotes the tourist industry.

家庭规模的变小和劳动力市场女性的增加使得今天的家庭更富裕,从而大大促进了旅游业。

Which 引出的是非限定性定语从句,修饰整个句子。如:

They turned a deaf ear to our demand, which enraged all of us very much.

他们对我们的要求置之不理,这使我们大家都非常生气。

9. that 用在以 it 引导的句子中,对某一成分加以强调,如:

It's you that are in charge of the daily routine of this travel agency.

是你负责这个旅行社的日常工作。(强调主语)

It was last summer vocation that I paid a visit to Tibet.

就在去年暑假我游览了西藏。(强调状语)

It is the tourist industry that we are mainly developing in the region of natural scenery.

旅游业是我们现在自然风景区的主要发展对象。(强调宾语)

10. seek the gratification of 寻求对……的满足

11. in turn 转而,依次,轮流

13. spectator sports 观众多的体育活动

14. by and large 大体上,基本上

15. self-esteem 自尊

16. Leisure can be defined as freedom from the necessity to labor.

空闲时间可以定义为必要劳动后的自由时间。

be defined as 表示被定义为。

17. discretionary income 无条件收益(个人收入中减去了必需支出)

Useful Expressions and Patterns

1. Are there any scenic spots here?

这儿有什么风景区吗?

2. Do you know any places of renown around here?

您知道这儿有什么名胜吗?

3. Are there any places of historic interest?

有什么历史遗迹吗?

4. Would you recommend some scenic spots to see here?

您能给我推荐一些这儿供游览的风景区吗?

5. I want to see all places of renown in Beijing.

我想游览北京的所有名胜。
6. I am going to the beach for a couple of weeks.
   我想去海滨过两个星期。
7. It's a tourist resort.
   这是一个旅游胜地。
8. The views from the hilltop are magnificent.
   从山顶看到的风景非常壮观。
9. I've never seen a waterfall like that before.
   我从来没见过那样的瀑布。
10. From up here we can have a bird's view of the city.
    从这儿我们可以鸟瞰这座城市。

Exercises

I. Answer the following questions according to text A.

1. Why do people like traveling so much?
2. What helps to stimulate the tourist industry both at home and abroad?
3. Can traveling relieve people from the strain and stress in our fast-developing modern society? Why?
4. In order to meet the needs of travelers' demands, what kind of special services should the travel agencies consider offering?
5. How can we improve the present situation of transportation and reduce the cost of travel?

II. Mark the following statements with "T" (True) or "F" (false) according to Text A.

1. "Self-actualization" may be achieved when a long-held dream comes true on a certain trip.
2. The most common reason for travel is associated with our physical well-being.
3. By learning about other cultures one can't also discover his own.
4. A combination of needs and desires has given impetus to of the largest industries today—the travel industry.
5. The increased time available began to be spent in the pursuit of recreation and pleasurable activities other than work.

III. Translation.

1. Translate the following sentences into Chinese.

1) Traveling offers chances to people who are eager to know other customs and culture, meanwhile, enriches their knowledge.
2) If you have been to an impressive place, you'll show more interest in the news and report about it.
3) Nowadays, some travel agencies provide new items, such as genealogical travel, gourmet travel, shopping travel etc.
4) In a word, leisure can help people free from the strain and nervousness from the society.

2. Translate the following into English.
1) 随着我们生活水平的提高,越来越多的人们在假期外出旅游。
2) 每周 40 小时的工作使人们有足够的时间享受各种娱乐和运动。
3) 今天在许多旅游景点,交通在很大程度上已经得到了改善,从而促进了当地的旅游业。
4) 通过旅游我们能够增长新的知识,结识新的朋友,品尝特色菜。

IV. Complete the following dialogue.

A: Excuse me, _____(有市内观光团吗)?

B: Certainly, we have a half-day tour and a full-day tour. Which one do you like?

A: _____(一日游的行程如何)?

B: It sets out at 8:00 a.m. and returns at 4:30 p.m.

A: It sounds _____ (不错). I will take it. By the way, _____(多少钱)?

B: It costs 100 dollars each person.

A: Can I _____ now (我现在可以预定吗)?

B: Of course.

V. Vocabulary and Structure.

1. Fill in the blank with the words or expressions given below. Change the form where necessary.

put more emphasis on; search for; give an impetus to; lead to; on a large scale; in general; by and large; be associated with; in turn; as far as...be concerned

1) I don't think that doing it like this _____ a good result.
2) Theory is based on practice and _____ serves practice.
3) To _____ pearls, the middle-aged man must dive again and again.
4) With the opening-up policy, we should _____ our export and import trade market.
5) China _____ always _____ the Great Wall by the foreign guests because

they think that it is a must for everyone to visit.
6) _____ I _____, some other arrangements would have been satisfactory.
7) In China _____ the number of traveling families greatly increasing.
8) Both the state schools and private ones _____ foreign languages and computers.
9) We must not only have a powerful regular army, but also organize contingents of the people's militia _____.
10) _____, we had a pleasant five-day trip to Thailand.

2. Match the following two columns.

A. 旅行方式　　　　　　　　a. human landscape
B. 休闲方式　　　　　　　　b. natural preserves
C. 休短假　　　　　　　　　c. a boom resort
D. 避暑胜地　　　　　　　　d. the national landscape
E. 自然景色　　　　　　　　e. take short-break holidays
F. 名胜古迹　　　　　　　　f. the mode of travel
G. 国家风景资源　　　　　　g. leisure time
H. 兴旺发达的旅游胜地　　　h. a summer resort
I. 人造景观　　　　　　　　i. historic interests
J. 自然保护区　　　　　　　j. natural scenery

3. Multiple Choice.
1) _____ has led to growing demand for tourism both at home and abroad and the expansion and improvement in associated facilities.
  A. Increased leisure time and improved incomes
  B. Low cost
  C. The economic recession
  D. A lot of holidays

2) Tourists take vacations not to _____.
  A. relax and have a good time
  B. learn another culture
  C. satisfy various needs and wants
  D. make profit

3) _____ is not psychological needs.
  A. Security　　　　　B. Activity
  C. Affection　　　　　D. Self-esteem

4) _____ Can be considered the end or goal of leisure.

A. Self-actualization B. Esteem
C. Aesthetics D. To know and understand

5) More than a hundred years ago, the main role of travel agents was to _____ .
   A. provide accommodation
   B. sell shipping and rail services
   C. find the attraction
   D. offer the amusement

6) If the agency is to succeed, _____ become paramount.
   A. good management
   B. good services
   C. both A and B
   D. intelligence of the agent

7) Travel agents are expected to cope with all the activities normally associated with the booking of travel, which will not include _____ .
   A. making reservation for all travel requirements
   B. maintaining accurate files on reservations
   C. issuing travel tickets and vouchers
   D. offering the free souvenir

8) As an area of scenic beauty attracts greater numbers of tourists, so the national landscape is lost to _____ .
   A. the summer season
   B. scenic countryside
   C. tourist development
   D. tourist needs

9) There is a widely known saying among the Chinese people —— "None of the Five Mountains need to be seen after coming back from _____ ."
   A. Hushan B. Hengshan
   C. Huangshan D. Taishan

10) The first travel agencies in China were established in _____ in _____ .
    A. Beijing...1923
    B. Tianjin...1930
    C. Nanjing...1920
    D. Shanghai...1923

VI. Situational Dialogue.

Make up a dialogue according to the given situation.

Imagine yourself to be a tourist guide with a group of foreign visitors to the city you like. Tell them what you know about the scenic spots in that city. Others will be the foreign visitors. And ask your guide where you can find the scenic spot you want.

VII. Mini Dialogues

Dialogue A

Scene: Accompanied by Li Hua, Mr. Smith and Mr. Green are going for sightseeing. They visit an ancient palace and a Chinese garden.

L= Li Hua　　　S = Mr. Smith　　　G = Mr. Green

L: Good morning. Tomorrow is Sunday. I'd like to invite you to go on an excursion.

S. Wonderful! Is there anything interesting to see in this city?

L: There are some famous historical sites and scenic spots to see in our city. I'm afraid two day's time isn't enough for us to see all the places of interests.

S: Let's make it a happy day. Would you like to be our tourist guide, Miss Li?

L: Certainly, I'd like to. We'll start tomorrow morning at 8:30, and I will come to your hotel at 8:20 to pick you up. Do you think you could manage to be ready then?

S&G: Yes, we think we can.

L: I'm afraid you should get up earlier than usual.

S: All right. I must get up a bit early.

L: See you tomorrow then.

S&G: See you tomorrow morning.

Dialogue B

S: What a beautiful site! Surrounded by mountains, I saw those nice buildings over there. Are they tombs?

L: No. It's an ancient king's palace.

S: What a magnificent ball! When was it built?

L: It was built at the beginning of the Ming dynasty, that is, in the early years of the fifteenth century.

S: But it's still in excellent condition, considering that it was built almost 600 years ago.

G: Could I take a few picture of it? I'm very much interested in picture Collecting.

I want to keep some pictures of ancient Chinese buildings.

L: Of course, you are welcome to do so. Now, there is a big lake behind the buildings.

G: It's nice there. Look, a lot of people are boating on the lake.

S: Look, all of the flowers are in full bloom, and the reflection of the pagoda in the lake looks very nice. What a charming place!

G: It's rather nice, isn't it? Perhaps, it's the best known scenic spot in the city.

L: Let's climb the hill. We can get a fine view of the from the hill top.

G: Oh, the views from the hill top are magnificent.

L: There is a beautiful garden over the hill.

G: Let's go there.

S: I'd like to, but I'm a bit thirsty.

L: There is a bar near the garden. We can get something to drink from the bar.

S: That's good, let's go.

L: Here we are. This is the bar. What would you like, Coca Cola, lemonade, orangeade or beer?

S: I'd like a bottle of beer.

G: I don't like beer. I'd like a can of Coca Cola.

L: (To the attendant) A bottle of beer and two cans of Coca Cola, please.

S: Let me settle the bill.

L: It's my treat. Let me pay.

(After drinking)

L: Shall we go in?

S: Yes. Let's go.

L: How do you like this garden?

S: It's a tiny garden, but it has a charm of its own.

L: This is a typical Chinese garden.

S: Quite charming and peaceful. One feels rather relaxed when sitting here, enjoying the beauty of the scenery, in the shade of these ancient trees.

G: I must take some pictures. This garden is worth looking at twice.

L: Welcome to visit our city once a year.

S: We'll come to China every year and visit one or two place each time.

VIII. Practical Writing.

Read the following notices, and write a notice about a bus tour to the Great Wall.

1
SUNRISE TOUR GROUP
Schedule for Tuesday, August 10

8:50 a.m. Meet in hotel lobby to board bus for the Summer Palace.
Lunch at the Summer Palace.
Quick stop at the Friendship Store for last-minute purchases.
4:30 p.m. Return to hotel.

Liu Xinhua,
Tour Guide
Monday, August 9

2
BUS TOUR

We are arranging for a bus tour to the Summer Palace on this SATURDAY, 24th September.

The bus will depart from the Beijing Hotel shortly after 8:30 a.m. and will return around 6 p.m., in time for dinner at the Hotel.

Lunch will be served at Listening to the Orioles Singing Restaurant In the Summer Palace.

There will be quick stops at the Haidian Free Market and the Beijing Zoo on our way back.

If you would like to join us, please place your name on the sheet on the Notice Board, or tell Mf. Wang Huaide or Xiao Liu at the front desk, and meet in the lobby at 8:30 a.m., SATURDAY, 24th September.

Cordially yours,
(Signature)
Hu Wendi,
Tour Guide

Text B The Travel Agency

Travel, whether for business or pleasure, requires arrangements. The traveler usually faces a variety of choices regarding transportation and accommodations, and if the trip is for pleasure, destinations, attractions, and activities. The traveler may gather information on prices, value, schedules, characteristics of the destination, and available activities directly, investing a considerable amount of time and money on long-distance telephone calls to complete the trip arrangements. Besides information, travelers' concerns may include time and money constraints and the desire for convenience, comfort, novelty, status, and variety. In order to solve all these problems, we need a travel agent who can meet the three basic needs common to all travelers: safety, reliability and accurate information by being an expert, knowledgeable in schedules, routings, lodging, currency, prices, regulations destinations and all other aspects of travel and travel opportunities.

The travel agency provides suppliers with a link to the public. On the one hand, provides a convenient place for the customers to purchase a variety of products, and on the other hand, saves the suppliers the trouble of setting up their own outlets or sending sales representatives all over the country. In the case of a travel agency, the suppliers consist of airlines, cruise ship lines, bus companies, railroads, hotels and motels, car rental firms, and wholesale tour operators; and the customers include vacation and leisure travelers, business travelers, and travelers visiting friends and relatives.

Retail travel agencies are differentiated from one another by the products and services offered, such as full-service travel agencies that offer all services and products related to international and domestic tourism, and, at the other extreme, limited-service agencies that may do only airline ticketing and offer discounted airfares as the primary basis for attracting clients. Travel agencies can also specialize according to market segments and product lines. Besides commercial agencies specializing in business, convention, and incentive travel, there are agencies serving holiday travelers, agencies for handicapped travelers, student travel agencies, ethnic agencies, and many others that provide services and products to particular market segments. In addition, some agencies specialize only in product line such as cruises, adventure tours, single destination travel, Oriental tours, or European tours.

The agency's service concept must be developed to give the clients what they want in a consistent manner over time. Standardization of operational procedures and analysis of the service delivery system are prerequisites to producing quality services. The end product of a satisfied customer must be achieved in line with the agency's financial goals in selling travel. After all is said and done, agents are salespeople and must generate sufficient sales to cover the costs of operations, including returns to owners. Cultivating long-term agent-client relationships is beneficial to both as an agency to develop new services or products to meet changing client needs.

Notes

1. gather information on 搜集关于……的信息
2. long-distance telephone call 长途电话
3. communicable disease 传染病
4. inbound tour operator 入境旅游经营者
5. in case of 就……来说
6. cruise ship 游船
7. retail travel agency 零售旅行社
8. car rental firm 汽车租赁公司
9. in line with 与……一致

Exercises: Answer the following questions according to Text B.

1. What shall a traveler think of before traveling?
2. What are the differences between full-service and limited-service travel agencies?
3. What are specialized travel agencies?
4. What are the basic needs common to all travelers?
5. In what areas should a travel agent be informed so as to be a qualified professional?

Text C Thomas Cook

Thomas Cook is a name of significance in the history of the travel industry. No textbook on travel retailers has ever failed to mention this name. As the first travel agent in England as well as in the world, he did some pioneering work in the field of travel retailing and contributed a lot to the growth of today's travel agent industry.

Born on November 22, 1808, at Melbourne, in Derbyshire, England, Thomas Cook can rightfully be recognized as the first rail excursion agent whose pioneering efforts were eventually to be copied widely in all parts of the world. By 1845 his company had come into operation. In 1856, Cook led his first Grand Tour of Europe and soon began conducting escorted tours. Besides conducting escorted tours, Thomas Cook took up the sale of domestic and overseas travel tickets in the early 1860s. His firm also took on military transport and postal services for England and Egypt during the 1880s.

On the whole, Cook was a man of vision in the world of travel. He recognized what economists refer to as the "elasticity of demand" of tourism. If prices can be brought down, more people will travel. So to help reduce prices he booked entire trains and blocks of hotel rooms to obtain a discount that he could pass on to his customers. He had close contacts with hotels, shipping companies and railways throughout the world, ensuring that he obtained the best possible services as well as cheap prices for the services he sold. The success of his operations was also due to the care he took in organizing his programs to minimize problems. By escorting his clients throughout their journeys abroad he took the worry out of travel for first-time travelers. He also facilitated the administration of travel by introducing, in 1867, the hotel voucher and in 1874 the circular notes, and so freed his travelers from worrying about the money they had to carry with them. By thus removing the worry of travel for the Victorians, he changed their attitudes to travel and opened up the market.

Thomas Cook died on July 18, 1892, in Leicester, Leicestershire at the age of 83. On his death the business passed to his only son, John Mason Cook. In 1931, the Thomas Cook Company merged with Wagons Lits, the operators of sleeping and dining ears on continental European express trains. Today, Thomas Cook remains one of the world's largest travel organizations; it has about six hundred offices and ten thousand employees around the world. However, Cook's true significance, according to Burkart and Medlik, was his invention of the excursion or holiday as a single transaction or package, rather than his establishment of a retail agency. His concept perfectly complemented the growth of the railways and later passenger shipping and brought organized travel to an increasingly large section of the public.

Notes

1. travel retailer 旅游零售商
2. excursion agent 短途旅行代理商
3. Grand Tour 大旅游
4. domestic tour 国内旅游
5. travel agent 旅游代理商

Exereises: Answer the following questions according to Text C.

1. Who is Thomas Cook?
2. When and where was Thomas Cook born?
3. When did Cook's company come into being?
4. What else did Cook do besides conducting escorted tours?
5. When and where did Cook die?

Unit 10   Tourist Shopping

Study structure

Text A (Intensive Reading): Tourist Commodities
Dialogues
New Words and Expressions
Exercises
Text B (Extensive Reading): Chinese Carpets
Text C (Supplementary Reading): How to Develop New Tourist Commodities

Summary of the Text

Tourist commodities are tangible objects bought by tourists on their tour. Tourists have special requirements for commodities in their assortment, quality, grade, design and choice of packaging or decoration. Tourist commodities have some differences from general merchandise. Chinese carpets are one kind of popular tourist commodities. Because of different times and places, the production and sales of tourist commodities fluctuate greatly. New tourist commodities will be constantly created.

Text A   Tourist Commodities

Tourist commodities are tangible objects bought by tourists on their tour. They consist largely of various art and handicraft articles, cultural relics and their imitations, native products, tourist souvenirs, tourists' daily use goods as well as other miscellaneous items of everyday life.

Tourist commodities manifest some differences from general merchandise. Viewed from the angle of production and operation, general merchandise is meant chiefly to serve the general public and to satisfy the needs of their daily lives, whereas tourist commodities are generally made to serve tourists. In other words, tourist commodities can be regarded as material products produced and operated by tourism destinations to meet the shopping needs of tourists from home and abroad while they are touring there.

As to the relationship between consumers and commodities, what tourists expect of tourist commodities are somewhat different what residents expect of general merchandise. The former usually have higher or more special requirements for commodities in their assortment, quality, grade, design and choice of packaging or decoration than the latter. Tourists usually lay great emphasis on the commemorative nature, artistic quality and practical applicability of tourist commodities. Commemorativeness is a very important property of tourist commodities. It can exhibit the distinguishing features of a tourism destination, the time when a tourist visits, and serve as evidence that a tourist has participated in certain tourist activities so that the commodities may bring back in the future good memories of the visit. The artistic quality refers to the overall novelty or beautiful design of a tourist commodity, which gives people esthetic enjoyment and endows the product with sentimental value. The practical applicability, however, indicates that tourist commodities must have actual usefulness to tourist. For instance, besides standing wear and tear, tourist commodities are also required to be light and handy, multi-functional and easy to carry.

Furthermore, the sale of tourist commodities has its own characteristics in display or the layout of stalls. Due to the fact that tourist commodities mainly serve tourists, their trading or the arrangement of the stalls are sometimes different from those of general merchandise whose main purpose is to satisfy the needs of local residents. Stores selling general merchandise are often set up near residential areas for the sake of residents' convenience. And they are usually well distributed. Stores handling tourist commodities, however, are usually put up in the commercially busiest sections of tourist cities, near places of historic interest or scenic beauty, and in hotels and shopping centers. This layout results from the special characteristics of tourist activities. Many regions of tourist destinations sell their tourist commodities to foreign tourists at the airports, wharves and stations of their ports of entry and exit. Foreign tourists who are departing can shop duty free at duty-free shops after customs inspection and before boarding, which is an international practice. Duty-free shops mostly conduct sales of tobacco and alcoholic drinks. In addition, they retail other high-grade goods, too. Since these commodities are exempt from import duties and sold at cheaper prices, they are bargains for tourists.

Lastly, tourist commodities differ from general merchandise in the fluctuating nature of their production and operation. The number of tourists has a direct impact on the production and sales of tourist commodities. And tourist flow is influenced by all kinds of factors in the economy, politics, natural conditions, social environments, etc. Furthermore, tourists are a flowing group unlike residents who are stable. Owing to the variation in tourist flow at different times and places, the production and sales of tourist commodities fluctuate greatly.

Dialogues

Dialogue A:

A: Where do you sell women's shoes?
B: It is on the third floor, madam.
A: Thank you, I also want to know if there is a fast food restaurant in your shop.
B: Yes, there is one. It's on the fifth floor.
A: Does the lift go up there?
B: Yes, madam, please take the lift marked 6.
A: It is very kind of you.
B: You are very welcome.

Dialogue B:

A: Sorry to interrupt you. Please take care not to make a mess when you are choosing goods.
B: Oh, I'm terribly sorry. But I could not find the candy I wanted to buy.
A: Maybe it is out of stock at the moment; why not choose another brand instead?
B: I am not sure whether the others are as good as the one I want to buy.
A: You may rest assured, in fact, all the goods for sale here are guaranteed of their quality.
B: In that case, I will have a try.

New Words an Expressions

1. commodity /kə'mɔditi/ n.商品
2. tangible /'tændʒəbl/ adj.可触摸的
3. relic /'relik/ n.纪念物,遗迹
4. imitation /ˌimi'teiʃən/ n.仿制品
5. souvenir /'suːvəniə/ n.纪念品
6. miscellaneous /ˌmisi'leinjəs/ adj.各种的
7. attribute /ə'tribjuːt/ n.归因,属性
8. merchandise /'məːtʃəndaiz/ n.商品
9. dual /'djuːəl/ adj.二重的

10. manifest /ˈmænifest/ v. 显示
11. whereas /wɛərˈæz/ conj. 而，却
12. somewhat /ˈsʌmwɔt/ adv. 稍微，有点
13. assortment /əˈsɔːtmənt/ n. 花色品种
14. commemorative /kəˈmemərətiv/ adj. 纪念的
15. applicability /æplikəˈbiliti/ n. 适用性
16. exhibit /igˈzibit/ v. 表现
17. novelty /ˈnɔvəlti/ n. 新奇的东西
18. esthetic /iːsˈθetik/ adj. 审美的
19. endow /inˈdau/ v. 赋予
20. indicate /ˈindikeit/ v. 显示，说明
21. furthermore /ˈfəːðəˈmɔː/ adv. 此外
22. layout /ˈleiaut/ n. 设计，布局
23. exempt /igˈzempt/ v. 使免除
24. bargain /ˈbaːgin/ n. 廉价货
25. fluctuate /ˈflʌktjueit/ v. 波动

Notes

1. consist...of 由……组成
2. in terms of 根据，按照
3. go through 经历，完成，经受
4. meet the needs of 满足……的需要
5. lay emphasis on 强调，着重于
6. for instance 例如
7. due to 因为，由于
8. for sake of 为了……
9. duty-free shop 出售给出境游客商品的零售免税商店
10. be exempted from 免于，被免除
11. owe to 应把……归功于
12. as well as 也，和
   We shall travel by night as well as by day. 我们将日夜赶路。
13. Viewed from the angle of production and operation, general merchandise is meant chiefly to serve the general public and to satisfy the needs of their daily lives, whereas tourist commodities are generally made to serve tourists.
   从生产和经营的角度看，一般商品主要为大众服务，满足他们的日常需

要,而旅游商品一般为游客服务。

view from the angle of 从……角度看

14. ... which gives people esthetic enjoyment and endows the product with sentimental value.

……给人以美的享受,并赋予了情感价值。

endow ... with ... 赋予某物……

15. Tourist commodities differ from general merchandise in the fluctuating nature of their production and operation.

旅游商品和一般商品在生产和经营的波动上也不同。

16. The number of tourists has a direct impact on the production and sales of tourist commodities.

游客的数量对旅游商品的生产和销售有直接的影响。

the number of ……数量,如:The number of books missing from the library is large.

图书馆遗失的书籍数量很大。

a number of 一些,如:A number of books are missing from the library.

图书馆里有一些书不见了。

Useful Expressions and Patterns

1. What style do you take?
   你喜欢什么式样的?

2. Is there anything else you'd like to buy?
   你还有什么要买的吗?

3. Do you have any cheaper ones?
   你们有便宜点的吗?

4. Have you got a bigger size?
   你们有尺寸大点的吗?

5. Can you recommend some to me?
   你能不能给我推荐一些?

6. It's of good quality.
   这是优品质。

7. It's the fashion now.
   现在正流行这种样式。

8. Sorry, but we don't have that in your size.
   对不起,我们没有您要的尺寸。

9. Sorry, but we're sold right out.
   对不起,全售完了。
10. Can you come down a bit?
    您可以便宜一点吗?

Exercises

I. Answer the following questions according to Text A.

1. What are tourist commodities?
2. In what sense are tourist commodities similar to general merchandise?
3. In what aspects do tourist commodities differ from general merchandise?
4. What are the three important characteristics of tourist commodities?
5. Why are duty-free tourist commodities warmly welcomed by tourists?
6. What leads to the fluctuating nature of tourist commodities in their production and operation?

II. Mark the following statements with "T" (True) or "F" (False) according to Text A.

1. Tourist commodities are tangible objects bought by tourists on their tour.
2. Tourist commodities have the dual qualities of both use value and value in the economic sense.
3. Tourist commodities are just like general merchandise.
4. Duty-free shops mostly conduct sales of tobacco and alcoholic drinks.
5. Stores selling general merchandise are often set up near residential areas for the sake of residents' convenience.

III. Translation.

1. Translate the following sentences into Chinese.
1) What tourists expect of tourist commodities are somewhat different from what residents expect of general merchandise.
2) Tourist commodities are also required to be light and handy, multi-functional and easy to carry.
3) Foreign tourists who are departing can shop duty free at duty-free shops.
4) The number of tourist has a direct impact on the production and sales of tourist commodities.

2. Translate the following into English.
1) 旅游商品具有使用价值和经济价值的双重特性。

2) 旅游商品是游客在旅途中购买的可触摸的物品。
3) 旅游商品的销售有它自身的特点。
4) 旅游商品能满足游客的购物需要。
5) 游客更看重旅游商品的纪念性、艺术性和实用性。

IV. Complete the following dialogue.

A: _____?

B: I am looking for a pair of black shoes.

A: _____?

B: Size nine.

A: I am afraid we _____ got any black shoes in that size at the moment, but we _____ some brown ones.

B: Hmm, have you got _____ kind?

A: _____ those shoes over there?

B: Well, that pair looks nice, _____?

A: Thirty-five dollars.

B: OK. Can I _____ please?

A: Certainly.

V. Vocabulary and Structure.

1. Fill in the blank with the words or expressions given below. Change the form where necessary.

have a better understanding; be outstanding for; be rich in; serve as; form a contrast of; be shrouded with; in addition; at the mouth of

1) What she said certainly _____ a means of getting attention.

2) Mother gave us sandwiches for our picnic and a bag of cookies _____.

3) They _____ the contribution they have made in every field of science, art, literature and sports.

4) The professor will make us _____ of the theory of relativity.

5) Our country _____ natural resources. We should make full use of them.

6) The exciting regatta will be held _____ the Lijiang River during the Dragon Boat Festival.

7) After the shower, the picturesque mountains _____ clouds and mists.

8) I am so sorry to say that the beautiful scenery _____ these polluted

places.

2. Match the following two columns.

A．购买力　　　　　　　a．tourism market
B．旅游经营商　　　　　b．travel retailers
C．旅游市场　　　　　　c．sales outlets
D．旅游零售商　　　　　d．source of revenue
E．销售网点　　　　　　e．travel product
F．收入来源　　　　　　f．return on sales
G．旅游产品　　　　　　g．purchasing power
H．销售回报　　　　　　h．tourist operator
I．工艺美术　　　　　　i．Terra cotta warriors and horses
J．兵马俑　　　　　　　j．arts and crafts

3．Multiple Choices.

1) The following persons who may be regarded as tourists in China are
    A．Members of foreign embassies in China
    B．Residents of the border area coming to China
    C．Overseas Chinese who come to China to visit relatives or friend
    D．Chinese who went abroad have come back

2) _____ is not main impulse driving the new tourism.
    A．New consumers
    B．New production practices
    C．Changes in the industry's from conditions
    D．New industry

3) The creation of income from tourism is closely bound up with _____.
    A．industry　　　　　B．investment
    C．employment　　　　D．the national economy

4) _____ can make the contribution to the balance of payments account in most countries with good tourism facilities.
    A．new attractions
    B．incoming tourism
    C．exchange rates
    D．industrial or agricultural export potential

5) China now ranked _____ in the world in terms of tourism dollars.
    A．six　　　　B．tenth　　　　C．ninth　　　　D．fifth

6) Tourism contributes to both and of the world's cultural herit _____ age.

A. Appreciation, structures

B. Contact, exchange

C. Interest, effect

D. Preservation, development

7) Tourists seek _____ as souvenirs or investments.

   A. instant culture

   B. cottage industries

   C. arts and cultural environment

   D. artifacts

8) _____ will be the primary tour product for the domestic tourist market in China.

   A. Long-stay travel

   B. Special interest and special events travel

   C. Business trip

   D. Sightseeing tour

9) The country from which the tourist comes is called _____ country.

   A. destination   B. origin

   C. vacation   D. native

10) _____ business means that the customers were satisfied and are coming back for more services or products.

   A. old   B. new

   C. repeat   C. recommended

VI. Situational Dialogue.

Make up a dialogue according to the given situation:

Mr. Thomson, an American traveler intends to buy some souvenirs and gifts for his friends and relatives. Supposing you are the shop assistant, recommend some souvenirs and gifts.

VII. Mini Dialogues.

Dialogues A

Scene: Mrs. Adams is standing by the Sweater Counter, amazed by the beautiful sweaters. A shop assistant comes to her help.

SA = Shop Assistant   A = Mrs. Adams

SA: Good afternoon, madam. Are you being helped?

A: No, I'd like to get a sweater in the new fashion. What style will be better on me?

SA: Your shape is so gracious, madam. Would you like to have sweater close-fitting or loose-fitting?

A: I like something loose-fitting.

SA: What do you think of this style?

A: This one? It's really elegant, but I'm afraid it's too narrow across the shoulders. I prefer a little wider.

SA: Yes, I see. Take that one then, madam. It's very loose in the waist and sleeves. It's quite popular with young people here.

A: What are these red flowers on the chest?

SA: They are plum flowers, the symbol of grace and nobility in Chinese culture.

A: That's wonderful! I'd take it. But I don't like the turtleneck. Could I have a V-neck sweater of the same color and with the same flowers?

SA: Of course, madam. Here you are.

Dialogues B

Scene: A lady and a man are in another section of the department store.

Shop Assistant = SA   A lady = L   A man = M

SA: What can I do for you?

L: We're just looking, thanks.

SA: Can I interest you in these silk scarves?

L: Oh, they are beautiful. Look at their designs.

M: Yes, they really are.

SA: They came in only yesterday, and sell very well.

L: May I have a look at the blue one.

SA: Sure, here you are. You can try it on.

L: Thanks. How do I look, darling?

SA: The scarf goes very well with your new coat.

A: How much does one cost?

L: 68 Yuan.

SA: That's a good bargain. Let's take it.

VIII. Practical Writing.

Read the two advertisements below and then try to write an advertisement:

Advertisement (1)

PALACE   DIEM

From the top terrace bar of the Grand Hotel Beijing

Sipping cocktail and viewing at the spectacular Forbidden City and Tian'anmen

Square, guests will be indulged in a dazzling vista created by the glazed roof tiles of the former emperor's residence,

Made to last an eternity.

If you want a deep insight of Chinese culture, take the opportunity to visit the Palace View Bar!

Business Hours: 6:00 p.m. ~ 10:00 p.m.

Venue: Tenth floor Terrace, Grand Hotel Beijing

For reservations, please contact

65137788 ext. 312 or 313

Grand Hotel Beijing

北京贵宾楼饭店

five stars

A member of

The Leading Hotels of the World

Advertisement (2):

The Capital Recreation Center

Latest 98 Brunswick bowling alley

Fully automatic computerized scoring

Newly upgraded pool, gym,

Billiard-room and games room

Brand new health center with sauna,

Steam bath, traditional Chinese

Massage, etc.

CAPITAL HOTEL

首都大酒店

3 Qian Men East, Beijing 100006, China Tel: (86-10) 65129988
Fax: (86-10) 65120309 E-mail Address: catlhtls public 3.bta.net.cn

Text B Chinese Carpets

As traditional products of arts and crafts, handmade carpets and tapestries have a long history. They are classified into several design-Beijing, Aesthetic, Floral, and Plain Embossed.

The "Beijing Design", reflecting a unique national and traditional style, is colorful and durable with fine workmanship. At the center of the "Beijing Design", there is a medallion, with flowers scattered around it, clouds at the corners and borders of different widths. This design symbolizes happiness, friendship, peace, wealth, longevity and good omens. The layout is solemn, showing the consciousness of the Chinese people in seeking stability and unity during the past several thousand years. The "antique-finished carpet" is even more fascinating. It looks smooth with its characteristic antiquity often arousing one's sentimentality.

Besides the "Beijing Design", there are also the "Aesthetic Design", a mixture of oriental and occidental arts, the "Floral Design", free and lively and the "Plain-Embossed Design" which is quite elegant. They are attractive enough to find quick buyers.

Internationally, Chinese carpets with Persian motifs do not sell so well as those from India, Pakistan or Iran does. These countries produce a type of cashmere silk woven carpets cheaper than those from China.

Overseas buyers usually buy Persian-style carpets from these countries and buy carpets with Chinese traditional motifs in China.

Woolen carpets made in China are hand-knotted ones with a pile Height of 1/4, 3/8, 1/2, 5/8 in. They are classified according to the number of lines of knots per unit of measurement. Most of the carpets have 70 to 300 lines. Those with lines up to 150 are top quality carpets and therefore are in greater demand than ever.

Carpets are generally offered in sizes of two by three to 12 by 22 Feet. Best selling sizes are two by four feet, three by five feet, four by Six feet and six by nine feet.

Wool from both the country's wool-producing areas and overseas is used. The best domestic wool comes from Xining, Tibet and Hexi. The imported wool is from Australia and New Zealand.

Shanghai is famous for its silk rugs and woolen carpets with floral designs. Rectangular, round, square and oval carpets are offered. They range from one-foot square to nine by twelve feet in size. Best selling sizes in U.S.A. and Western Europe are six by nine and nine by twelve feet.

Notes

1. Plain-Embossed 素凹凸式

2. good omen 良好的预兆
3. arouse one's sentimentality 唤起人们的情怀
4. Persian motif 波斯风格
5. according to the number of lines of knots per unit of measurement 以单位尺寸的道数来分档的
6. Hexi 河西走廊

Exercises: Answer the following question according to Text B.
1. How many kings of carpets?
2. Say something about the several designs of the carpet.
3. Which carpets are in greater demand?
4. What are the best selling sizes in the U.S.A. and Western Europe?
5. What are the best sell?

Text C How to Develop New Tourist Commodities

Apart from developing and improving existing tourist commodities, tourist enterprises should aim at developing new products. There are three types of new tourist commodities: improved products, renovated products, and brand-new products. Improved products are those whose quality is improved, specifications and models diversified, and design and color retrofitted by means of improved technology and by perfecting the functions of the existing tourist commodities. Tourist clothing is a case in point. Renovated products are new tourist commodities made in the pattern of the original products, but with some new technology and new materials. Consequently, the functions of the commodities are greatly enhanced. Brand-new products are products made with new principles, new techniques, new technology, new materials, and new design.

There are four basic requirements for developing new tourist commodities. First, new tourist commodities should have their own characteristics. That is, the products must maintain originality, new properties and new uses. Second, the new commodities must have market ability. New products are not developed merely for new markets. It is recommended that a survey or investigation of the demand on the market be made to get reliable information before mass production of a certain new product. Third, new products should be developed on the basis of the means and capabilities of an enterprise. In other words, the enterprise has to make its plan of developing new products according to its production scale, financial capacity, material resources, and availability of manpower. Fourth, developing new products what must have profitability as its prerequisite. In developing new products what must be taken into full consideration is the practical ratio in the future. It is desirable of all enterprise to obtain great economic gains out of low expenditures. To achieve this goal, thought must be given not only to short-term gains but also sustainable profitability.

The marketing of tourist commodities has become a means to promote cultural exchanges among nations. Therefore, nowadays, many countries are doing their best to develop tourist commodities by utilizing their unique resources, and assisting or increasing sales of this king of commodities so as to advance the development of their tourism industry and even their economy as a whole.

Notes

1. apart from 除……以外
2. brand-new product 崭新的产品
3. by means of 用,凭借
4. take into full consideration 对……加以充分考虑

Exercises: Decide whether the following statements are True of False.

1. There are three types of new tourist commodities: improved products, renovated products, and brand-new products.
2. There are four basic requirements for developing new tourist commodities.
3. The new commodities must have market ability.
4. New products are developed merely for the sake of developed.
5. New products should be developed on the basis of the means and capabilities of an enterprise.

APPENDIX 1
key to the Exercises

参 考 答 案

Unit 1

Text A

I. Omitted

II. 1.F   2.F   3.T   4.F   5.F

III.

1. 1) 美国幅员辽阔,如果您想参观50个州的大部分的话,那么乘坐飞机旅游是惟一切合实际的办法。

    2) 飞机旅行不贵,航班多,衔接快。

    3) 乘坐国内航线,如果你已经买了机票并订了座位,那么您只需提前一个小时到达机场便可。

    4) 航空公司在大部分的商业机场雇佣大量的员工,其大部分的雇员在集散大楼工作。

    5) 大部分航空公司都有计算机系统快速打印机票和查看航班空座。

2. 1) What date and what number of the flight do you want to book?

    2) There is a flight from here to Beijing every two hours.

    3) Please remember to confirm your flight.

    4) Economy fare for one-way trip from to New York to Shanghai is $800.

    5) Please arrive at the airport one hour before departure.

IV.

1. A: a domestic flight timetable

    B: Here you are

    B: It only takes one hour

2. A: How much is the fare

    A: gasoline   tolls   a round trip ticket to Tianjin

3. A: direct flights

    B: You're welcome

4．A：Domestic Reservations

　　B：make a reservation to Haikou for tomorrow

　　A：first-come, first-served

V．

1．1) complex　　2) function　　3) additional　　4) briefing

　　5) rewarding　　6) board　　7) demonstration　　8) reservation

　　9) airborne　　10) crew

2．A—d　B—e　C—c　D—f　E—b　F—a

3．1) C　2) B　3) B　4) C　5) B

VI．Omitted

VIII．Omitted

Unit 2

Text A

I．Omitted

II．1.T　2.F　3.F　4.F　5.F

III．

1.1) 当乘客下了飞机的时候，玛丽和约翰走上前去迎接他们。

　2) 在航空集散大楼里有入境处、海关、行李间，还有许多航空公司设立的售票、订票处。

　3) 他们将竭力快捷地为游客服务。

　4) 请各位准备好您们的入境卡、护照以及相关文件。

　5) 游客和其他来访者需要填写入境信息卡以便解释入境理由。

2．1) Have you got anything to declare, sir?

　2) I'm sorry, sir, but in this item you will have to pay import duties.

　3) Have a good stay in Beijing.

　4) Could you put that suitcase on the counter and open it, please?

　5) How long do you plan to stay in Shanghai?

IV．A：Your passport

　　A：Do you have anything to declare

　　B：Some bottles of perfume and some bottles of whisky

　　A：open your suitcase for examination

　　B：What can I do with them

　　A：fill in this foreign currency declaration form

V.
1. 1) host 2) tone 3) custom 4) influence 5) salary
   6) fortune 7) honest 8) in advance 9) out of style
   10) overnight
2. A—d B—e C—f D—c E—b F—g G—a
3. 1) C 2) C 3) C 4) D 5) A 6) A 7) B 8) D 9) A 10) A
VI. Omitted
VII. Omitted
VIII. Omitted

Unit 3

Text A

I. Omitted

II. 1. F 2. T 3. T 4. F 5. F 6. F

III. Translation

1. 1) 在近代,汽车和飞机也已经成为娱乐方面的主要交通形式。
   2) 但如果不是因为大大降低了旅行开销,或是维也纳会议没有为人们在稳定的和平环境中赏景奠定基础,新的旅游观光者们是不大可能有出门旅行的机会的。
   3) 黄金时代是繁华和成功的时代,但也是价值更新的时代。即将到来的旅游大繁荣时期可能也是如此。
   4) 在许多国家,夏季是传统的度假季节。例如在美国,人们在炎热的月份里离家前往山里或海边的旅游胜地。
   5) 很多观光旅游只限于对本地景点的半日游或一日游。

2. 1) The first day of the lunar year is the traditional Chinese festival—the Spring Festival. It is the time of the family reunion.
   2) Festivals are also the lucky days for wedding, for people may have plenty of time to enjoy the ceremony.
   3) On the evening of the Mid-Autumn Festival, family members get together to worship the moon while tasting the moon cakes and enjoying the family harmony.
   4) The Water-Sprinkling Festival is the festival for Dai minority.
   5) The ninth day of the ninth lunar month is Aged People's Day, also called Chong Yang Festival. A series of activities are going on to show respect and

concern for the old in our society.

6) Unlike the others over the world, Chinese people adopt the solar calendar as well as the lunar calendar.

Ⅳ. about   how to   that's   details   when   New Year   Will it   Sichuan
good at   How much   the end   sure   meet people   hear it

Ⅴ.

1. 1)takes on   2) carries out   3) called upon   4) In addition   on occasion
5) is related to   6)in that sense   7) have effect on   8) in turn   9) take care of

2. A—j   B—c   C—d   D—b   E—f   F—h   G—a   H—i   I—e
   J—g

3. 1)C   2)B   3)B   4)B   5)B

Ⅵ. Omitted

Ⅶ. Omitted

Ⅷ. Omitted

Text B

1.T   2.F   3.T   4.T   5.F

Text C

Omitted

Unit 4

Text A

Ⅰ. Omitted

Ⅱ. 1.F   2.F   3.T   4.F   5.F

Ⅲ. Translation

1. 1) 大多数情况下,书写地址按如下顺序:首先房屋号码,然后是街道、城市、州、邮政编码,最后写国家名。

2) 传统说来,结尾套语应写在正文下方,信纸右面和上面日期对齐的位置。

3) 每个结构完整的商务信件都应包括十个基本组成部分,即,信头、信内地址、称呼、事由主题、正文、结尾套语以及发信者的签字、身份、头衔等。

4) 通过邮局安全投递有两种方式:挂号邮件和保证邮件。

5) 一天中,你可能几次地通过电话询问旅行事宜。

2. 1) We are still widely using letters for business communication because of the safety and low cost.
   2) E-mails enable indiriduals and companies to communicate reliably, cheaply, efficiently, conveniently around the globe.
   3) People in the information age are making full use of telex, fax and e-mail to convey the latest news.
   4) It is predicted that various communication systems will develop more quickly and widely in all kinds of fields in the coming years.
   5) keep unrelated matlers out of your business lethers so as not to make a misunderstanding.
   6) In different couptries, the expression of the date is also not the same while writing a letter heading, so don't be confused with the usage in dating letters.

Ⅳ. G: send this parcel to my mother in the United States
   C: How do you like to send it, by air or by surface
   C: About two to three months
   G: I want it to arrive in the U.S.
   G: How much faster will it be by air
   G: I'll send it by air then
   C: Could you fill out this form, please
   C: Can you open the parcel for our inspection, please
   G: Here is one hundred note
   C: change and your receipt

Ⅴ. 1. 1) Generally speaking 2) adopted   3) was located in   4) was divided into   5) derived... from   6) gave priority to   7) found out   8) made a reservation   9) Up to   10) speed up
2. A—e B—c C—j D—g E—h F—b G—i H—d I—a J—f
3. 1) A   2) D   3) C   4) A   5) B
Ⅵ. Omitted
Ⅶ. Omitted
Ⅷ. Omitted
Text B   1) F   2) T   3) F   4) T   5) F
Text C   Omitted

Unit 5

Text A

Ⅰ. Omitted.
Ⅱ. 1. F   2. T   3. F   4. F   5. T   6. F
Ⅲ. Translation

1. 1) 由于旅游必须离家外出,这种大规模行业的发展就有赖于迅速发展而又价格便宜的现代交通工具。

   2) 旅游业并不是一个单一的实体,它由许多为旅客提供各种服务的多种不同企业所组成,如交通运输业、住宿业、饮食业、旅行社经营和旅行代理商等。

   3) 普通类型的旅游可以分为两种。一种是以一个旅游胜地旅馆为目的地的假日包价旅游。第二种是有导游的旅游,以观光或其他一些吸引人的特殊东西为其特点。

   4) 为来宾办理住宿手续并为他们安排房间的是前台服务员。

   5) 顾客一到饭店,前台服务员即查对他是否曾经预定房间。如果顾客事先未订房间,则需了解是否还有空房。

2. 1) Hotels are divided into four major classifications: the commercial hotel, the resort hotel, the motor hotel and the residential hotel.

   2) A deluxe hotel will try its best to offer the guests the most comfortable environment and convenient equipment.

   3) The Food and Beverage Department plays a very important role in the hotel management.

   4) Some hotels are closed during the "off season" and reopen at the peak season in order to reduce the expenses.

   6) In fact, the services a motel provides are very similar to those of other hotels.

   7) A hotel is mainly made up of a front office, a house keeping department, a food and beverage department, a business center and so on.

Ⅳ. B: coming   recommended your hotel
   A: would you be wanting to stay
   A: would you be planning to arrive
   A: a single room or a double
   A: offer you a single
   B: what is

A：$120
B：book（have a reservation）
A：what name is it
A：book that for you
A：You're very welcome

V. 1. 1) on the premises   2) for pleasure   3) developed the habit of
   4) confirmation   5) cashier   6) reserved   7) direct to   8) illustrate
   9) are similar to   10) describe
2. A—c B—d C—i D—g E—a F—j G—e H—b I—f
   J—h
3. 1) B 2) B 3) D 4) B 5) A 6) B 7) A 8) D 9) B
   10) D
VI. Omitted
VII. Omitted
VIII. Omitted
Text B   Omitted
Text C   1. F   2. F   3. T   4. F   5. T   6. F

Unit 6

Text A

I. Omitted
II. 1. F   2. F   3. T   4. F   5. T   6. T
III. Translation
1. 1) 旅游代理商一定要随时了解政府有关国际旅游方面经常变化的规定（签证和健康规定、关税信息、机场税等），以便告诉旅游者准确情况。
   2) 前台服务员查明确有房间后，请顾客在卡上填好姓名、家庭住址和其他情况。
   3) 导游用事先准备好的解说词向游客介绍将要游览的景点，但他也必须回答各种提问和处理人们可能发生的问题。
   4) 旅客们进入海关后必须填报一份"旅客行李申请单"，此份申报单由旅客自己保留，在离开中国时，交与海关检查。
   5) 所有的酒店员工应该记住：只有在宾客得到极大程度的满意时，宾馆才能成功地获得更多的经济效益。
   6) 旅游服务中心通过做广告和进行一些特别的促销活动来推销或组织

去目的地国的旅行。

2. 1) I particularly wish to become a professional hotel manager.

   2) Can you fix me up with a room attendant?

   3) I got a degree in Hotel Management and took a computer course.

   4) Management contract is the contract which is signed between hotel chains and the owners of a hotel.

   5) Other chain hotels that operate on a worldwide basis are Sheraton, Inter-Continental, Trust Houses, Forte, Hilton International and Romada Inns.

   6) Guests change some money and check out at the cashier's desk of the hotel.

IV. C: can   do

   M: check

   C: Tell   your   room   leave

   C: moment   in

   C: sign   different   them   make   expenses

   C: are   you   going   to   pay

   C: waiting   enjoyed   a pleasant

V. 1. 1) made a impression on   2) etiquette   3) the mutual   4) at a good pace   5) have a sentimental attachments for   6) assured of   7) contributes to   8) adept   9) laid   emphasis   10) embodies

2. A—f   B—h   C—a   D—j   E—b   F—c   G—d   H—e   I—g   J—i

3. 1) B   2) C   3) A   4) D   5) C   6) C   7) A   8) C   9) B   10) D

VI. Omitted.

VII. Omitted.

Text B   Omitted

Text C   1. F   2. T   3. F   4. T   5. T   6. F

Unit 7

Text A

I. 1. Its flavor is fantastic and the techniques are delicate.

   2. Eight.

   3. It is clean, pure and not greasy, and it is characterized by its emphasis on aroma, freshness, crispness and tenderness.

4. Gongbao Diced Chicken, Twice Cooked Pork, Mapo Beancurd.

5. It consist of dishes of Hangzhou, Ningbo and Shaoxing.

II. 1.T 2.F 3.F 4.T 5.T 6.F 7.F 8.F

III.

1. 1) 中国菜以其美妙的味道和精致的技艺而闻名世界。

   2) 山东菜由济南菜和胶东菜组成,味道清爽、纯正、不油腻,以强调香、鲜、脆、嫩为主要特点。

   3) 四川菜以辛辣、刺激的口味为主要特点,口味多样,主要强调使用辣椒和花椒粉。

   4) 最常用的是蒸和炒,来保持原料的自然口味。

   5) 它不仅选料精良,而且以刀工精细、造型美观、制作精美、赏心悦目而闻名。

2. 1) In general, Chinese cuisine can be divided into eight styles of regional dishes.

   2) Fistulous onion and garlic are frequently used as seasonings in Shandong dishes.

   3) In Sichuan dishes, wild edible herbs and the meat of domestic animals and birds are often chosen as ingredients.

   4) The flavor of Huaiyang cuisine is light, fresh and sweet and its presentation is delicately elegant.

   5) Often ham will be added to improve taste and rock candy can be added to gain freshness in Anhui cuisine.

IV. 1. A: May I take your ordr

   A: Our specialties are

   2. A: How would you like your steak done, well-done, medium, or rare

   B: I'd like it well done please

   3. B: I'd like to book a table for two this evening

   A: When should we expect you

V.

1. 1) edible 2) technique 3) be divided into 4) consists of 5) flavors

   6) aroma 7) is characterized by 8) originated from

2. A—d B—f C—a D—g E—h F—b G—e H—j I—c J—i

VI. G = Guest   W = Waitress

   W: Good evening. Can I take your order now, sir?

   G: We are still looking at the menu. We don't know much about Chinese food. Could you recommend the specialties of your restaurant?

W: Our specialties are Baked Beef on an Iron Plate, Chicken Cubes with Chilli Peppers, Sweet and Sour Crispy Fish, and Wine Preserved Crabs.

G: Baked Beef on an Iron Plate, and Sweet and Sour Crispy Fish. What vegetables do you have?

W: We have various vegetable dishes, Fish-flavored Eggplants, Soft-fried Fresh Mushrooms, Stir-fried Mashed potato. They all taste good.

G: We want to order Fish-flavored Eggplants.

W: Which soup do you like?

G: Tomato and Egg Drop Soup.

W: Any more?

G: No more, thank you.

W: You're welcome.

VII. Omitted

VIII.

假日大酒店欢迎各位贵宾光临	
宴会菜单	
MENU	
Steamed Fish-flavored Prawns	鱼香旱蒸虾
Sweet and Sour Crispy Fish	糖醋脆皮鱼
Fried Chicken with Spicy Sauce	油淋香鸡
Hot and Peppery Beef	麻辣牛肉
Pork Ribs with Fermented Soybean Sauce	豉汁排骨
Sliced Pock with Garlic	蒜泥白肉
Soft-fried Winter Bamboo Shoots	软炸冬笋
Dry Fried Kidney Beans	干煸四季豆
Braised Assorted Vegetables	什锦素烩
Cauliflower with Cream	奶油菜花
Fish Balls in Consomme	清汤鱼丸

Unit 8

Text A

I. 1. Five. They are green tea, black tea, Wulong tea, compressed tea and jasmine

tea.
2. Green tea keeps the original colour of the tea leaves without fermentation during processing, while black tea needs fermentation before baking.
3. Longjing of Zhejiang province, Maofeng of Huangshan Mountain in Anhui proivce and Biluochun in Jiangsu province.
4. It is good for transport and storage. Most of compressed tea is in the form of bricks.
5. Drinking tea can help people keep fit; tea may help resolve fat and promote digestion; it is rich in vitamins; it helps to discharge nicotine out of the system; it can help drunken people sober up.

II. 1. F   2. T   3. T   4. F   5. F

III.
1. 1) 尽管英语单词"tea"的发音与普通话"茶"(cha)的发音不一样,但是它的发音与厦门方言"茶"的发音相似。
   2) 按照不同的生产工艺,中国茶可分为五种：绿茶、红茶、乌龙茶、压缩茶(砖茶)和茉莉花茶。
   3) 乌龙茶的工艺介于绿茶和红茶之间,是经过部分发酵后生产出来的。
   4) 大多数的压缩茶都制成砖形,因此一般被称为砖茶,尽管有些时候也被制成蛋糕或碗的形状。
   5) 据报道,经常饮用过浓的茶水对有些人来说会导致心脏和血压紊乱,而且会使年轻人的牙齿变黑。

2. 1) Tea growing in China can be traced back to more than 2 000 years ago.
   2) Brick tea is good for transport and storage and is mainly supplied to the remote area.
   3) Jasmine tea is a favorite with the northerners of China.
   4) People who live mainly on meat often drink tea to promote digestion.
   5) I'm rather bored than tired.

IV.
1. W: What would you like to drink
   G: I'll have a cocktail
   W: Which would you like
2. W: May I help you
   G: What happened to my breakfast
   W: I'm sorry for the delay
   W: Would you please wait a little longer

V.

1. 1) derive from   2) be traced back to   3) keep fit   4) rather than   5) rich in   6) sobers up   7) The more the more   8) resulted in

2. 1) classify   2) compressed   3) favorites   4) necessities   5) resolved   6) minority   7) was discharged   8) yield

3. A—h   B—e   C—f   D—a   E—b,d   F—c,g

VI.

W = Waitress   G = Guest

G: Room service. May I help you?

W: Yes, you can. I need more wine. There isn't any more in my mini-bar.

G: Your name and room number, sir.

W: I'm John White in 615.

G: OK. Six-one-five. I'll send some more wine. Will there be anything else, sir?

W: No. Thank you very much.

VII. Omitted

VIII.

You are cordially invited by
The presient of Hongxing Company Mr Li Ming
To attend an anniversary Reception
At Longjiang Restaurant,
At 11:30 a.m. on Sunday, May 15, 2005

R.S.V.P.

8657721

Text B

1. 20 different types of ales, lagers, stouts and bitters; wine, and liquor; some non-alcoholic drinks.

2. Darts, billiards and skittles.

3. No, there isn't.

4. No, there isn't.

5. We can catch the barman's eye or have a slightly anxious, hopeful or expectant expression.

6. No, it isn't.

Text C

1. In Tang Dynasty.

2. Brick tea.

3. Chestnut paste, sesame powder, peanuts, melon seed kernels, pine nuts, eggs and salt.
4. A dough of roasted Qingke barley flour and tea.
5. The cup can be drained and the dregs thrown on the ground.
6. Mongolian snacks, such as fried rice, milk cakes, deep fried milk products and boiled mutton.

Unit 9

Text A

Ⅰ. Omitted

Ⅱ. 1. T   2. T   3. F   4. T   5. T

Ⅲ. Translation

1. 1) 旅游给人们提供了了解其他风俗文化的机会,同时也丰富了他们的知识。
   2) 如果你去过某一个给你留下深刻印象的地方,你将会对有关这个地方的新闻报道更感兴趣。
   3) 现在有些旅行社推出新的项目,例如:寻根旅游、美食旅游、购物旅游等。
   4) 总地说来,休闲帮助人们摆脱来自社会的压力和紧张。

2. 1) With the development of our life, more and more people will go traveling on their holidays.
   2) The forty-hour workday in a week makes people have enough time to enjoy different entertainments and sports.
   3) Today at many scenic spots, transportation has been bettered on a large scale; hence it promoted the local tourist industry.
   4) We can enlarge our knowledge, make new friends and taste the specialties through traveling.

Ⅳ. A: do you have city tours
   A: What is the schedule of the full-day tour
   A: not bad   how much
   A: have a reservation

Ⅴ.

1. 1) will lead to   2) in turn   3) search for   4) give an impetus to   5) is associated with   6) As far as   am concerned   7) in general   8) put

more emphasis on   9) on a large scale   10) By and large

2. A—f   B—g   C—e   D—h   E—j   F—i   G—d   H—c   I—a   J—b

3. 1) A   2) D   3) C   4) A   5) B   6) C   7) D   8) C   9) C   10) D

Ⅵ. Omitted

Ⅶ. Omitted

Text B   Omitted

Text C   Omitted

Unit 10

Text A

Ⅰ. Omitted

Ⅱ. 1. T   2. T   3. F   4. T   5. T

Ⅲ. Translation

1. 1) 游客对旅游商品的期望和居民对普通商品的期望有些不同。

   2) 旅游商品也需要轻便、多功能和便携。

   3) 外国游客在离开前可以到免税商店购买免税商品。

   4) 游客的数量对旅游商品的生产和销售有直接的影响。

2. 1) Tourist commodities have the dual qualities of both use value and value in the economic sense.

   2) Tourist commodities are tangible objects bought by tourists on their tour.

   3) The sales of tourist commodities has its own characteristics.

   4) Tourist commodities can meet the shopping needs of tourists.

   5) Tourists lay great emphasis on the commemorative nature, artistic quality an practical applicability of tourist commodities.

Ⅳ. A: What can I do for you

   A: What size do you want

   A: haven't   have

   B: any other

   A: What about

   B: how much do they cost

   B: try them on

V.
1. 1) served as   2) in addition   3) are outstanding for   4) have a better understanding   5) is rich in   6) at the mouth of   7) are shrouded with   8) forms a contrast of
2. A—g   B—h   C—a   D—b   E—c   F—d   G—e   H—f   I—j   J—i
3. 1) C   2) D   3) C   4) B   5) C   6) D   7) D   8) D   9) B   10) C
V. Omitted
VI. Omitted
VIII. Omitted
Text B   Omitted
Text C   1. T   2. T   3. T   4. F   5. T

APPENDIX 2
Chinese Translation of Texts A (Unit 1 ~ Unit 10)

参 考 译 文

第1单元 预定机票

Text A

航空旅行

飞机在远距离旅行中越来越普遍。越来越多的人喜欢乘坐飞机旅行，是因为它快捷、安全。在航空旅行服务的方方面面中，航空公司起了很大的作用。

航空公司，特别是国际航空公司，是一个具有许多复杂功能的庞大机构。它有售票和订票代理商、机场服务人员、运货服务人员、机修工、饮食服务人员、飞行员，以及飞机上的工作人员等。

机长或飞行员，就像船长一样，自始至终负责整个飞机的航行。他的助手是副驾驶员，也是第二指挥员。还有一位飞行员兼飞机工程师，他负责所有机械设备的正常运转。如果是远程飞行，也许还会有另一位被称为二副的飞行员。飞行人员只在飞机的座舱里工作。所以，乘客很少见到他们，但机长会通过扬声器向乘客说话。他通常是在起飞后不久向乘客问好，然后对有关航行中的一些景点的地理位置和天气情况作大致介绍。

半个世纪以来，空姐的工作一直被认为是一份很刺激、令人兴奋而又报酬丰厚的职业，虽然这职业通常被认为是女士的工作，但决不只限于她们。男士也在这个日益发展的领域里起着重要的作用。

对于全体机务人员来说，在登机前要对飞机做许多准备工作。到机场签到后，就要与机组的其他人员碰头，参加由机长组织的基本情况介绍会。在会上，机长会告知飞行计划、天气情况，以及其他有关影响饮食服务的因素。在起飞前半小时，乘客开始登机。飞机服务人员欢迎乘客登机，并帮助他们找到座位，随后会有一些欢迎词、登机通知以及紧急设备运用的示范表演。起飞前，空姐所做的最后一件事就是检查乘客的安全带。

飞机一起飞，舱内服务人员就变得特别忙碌。她们的工作大部分是供应乘客饭食与饮料,还要详细解说需要注意的事项。当飞机快到目的地时,飞机事务长就会通知有关着陆程序,机内服务人员检查乘客和机舱是否已准备好着陆。飞机着陆后,他们帮助乘客下机,并和乘客告别。

对话:预订机票

对话 A

甲:早晨好,美国航空公司,玛丽小姐为您服务。

乙:你好,我想预订一张后天也就是6月6日到纽约的机票。

甲:请稍候。让我为您查一下。(片刻之后)让您久等了。很抱歉,我们那天的票全都订完了。下一次航班是6月7日周日上午八点起飞。我能为您预订这次航班吗?

乙:好的。

对话 B

甲:您好,加拿大航空公司为您服务。

乙:您好,我想预订一张机票。

甲:您想要头等舱还是经济舱?

乙:经济舱。

甲:您可以在我们的任何一家办事处购买机票。感谢您致电加拿大航空公司。

乙:谢谢。

对话 C

甲:我想取消我3日去北京的125次航班的预订票。我的名字是托尼辛普森。

乙:请稍等。谢谢,让您久等了。我已经取消了您的预订票。我可以为您预订其他的机票吗?

甲:不用了,谢谢。

乙:我明白了。如果您还想预订机票的话,请再次致电我们。谢谢您来电英国航空公司。

第2单元 海关

Text A

海关

当乘客下了飞机的时候,玛丽和约翰走上前去欢迎他们。玛丽和约翰是乘客服务代理,他们代表他们国家的航空公司为乘客服务。

"欢迎，"约翰说，"我们很高兴各位来到我们国家。如果您愿意的话，我们可以带您去入境处。"

下了飞机的乘客随着乘客服务代理来到一座很大航空集散楼。

在集散楼里，有入境处、海关、行李间，还有许多航空公司设立的售票和订票处。

除此之外，在大楼里还有候机厅、商店、餐馆和其他一些为乘客提供服务的设施。

当乘客跟随着玛丽在较长的大楼走廊里走着的时候，克林顿夫人问："入境要花很长时间吗？"

玛丽回答道："我想不会的。那里有很多的移民官员。他们会尽力快捷地为乘客服务的。"

克林顿先生说："很好，我们已经厌倦被困在飞机里，我们非常希望能尽快看看你们的国家。"

当乘客走到入境处的时候，看到在高高的柜台前已经有很多人在那里排队等候。每个柜台后，坐着一名移民官。在那里高挂着一副标志牌：游客—参观客。玛丽示意克林顿夫妇去那个柜台。

当夫妇俩排队之后，玛丽说，"不会花很长的时间。请准备好入境卡、护照和其他相关文件。希望你们在我们国家玩得愉快。"

文件指的是官方发放的证件。护照是持有人离开和再次进入国家的许可文件。国家发放护照给其国民。克林顿先生随身带着他和夫人的护照。

在入境处，乘客服务代理回答乘客的问题并帮助他们排好队。有些人是度假回来，他们是本国人或者是定居者。

尽管"入境"意味着要进入这个国家居住，但是所有入境者必须通过入境处检查，无论其呆多久。

入境官员要检查他们的证件和身份。这样的话，这个国家就清楚入境者的情况和他们来自的国家。游客和其他的来访者要填写入境卡以解释其入境理由。

欲永久居住在一个国家的人被称为移民。有时，他们和这个国家的国民结婚。他们希望居住在这个国家但保留自己国家的国民身份。有些人在居住一段时间之后，打算成为这个国家的公民。无论怎样，他们都必须出示专门的证件来解释其意图。

想永久居住在某个国家的移民者常常要由一位该国国民推荐。这位国民要对移民者负责。国民能够承诺移民者不会成为这个国家的负担。另外，他也需要保证移民者不是从另一个国家逃出来的罪犯。

移民者和回国的本国国民在入境处要多花一点的时间。这就是为什么常常有不同的几组排队。移民官倒是很希望游客能尽早地通过入境处。

对话：通关

对话 A

A：我可以看看您的护照吗？

B：当然可以，给你。

A：您打算在纽约呆多久？

B：大约一个月。

A：您有什么东西要申报的吗？

B：是的，我买了一块手表和一件衣服。

A：您可以携带一百美元的免税品，因此您无须为您的手表和衣服保税。

B：谢谢。

对话 B

A：您能把您的手提包放在柜台上打开吗？里面装了什么？

B：一包绿茶和一些香蕉。

A：很抱歉，先生。您不可以带新鲜的水果进入美国。我得没收。

B：哦，太糟糕了。

对话 C

A：您打算呆多久？

B：大约一个月。

A：您此行的目的是什么？

B：我要看看我的朋友。

A：我可以看看您的包吗？能打开吗？

B：当然。

A：这台相机是送您朋友的礼物吗？

B：不，是我个人用的。

第 3 单元 娱乐活动

Text

现代生活

现在，在中国人们每周通常工作 40 小时。这给中国人提供了更多的娱乐时间，比如、钓鱼、游泳、滑雪、打保龄球、摄影、园艺等，这些是比较时尚的娱乐休闲方式。

周末休息两天或是五一和十一的长假给人们提供了更多的时间去做自

己想做的事。许多中国人都利用这些时间去旅游,去欣赏祖国名胜和自然奇观。中国有许多这样的旅游景点。每年都有成千上万的人去各种国家公园游玩,在那里人们可以游泳、钓鱼,参加各种各样的活动。目前,中国有许多娱乐休闲场所,使人们能够缓解疲劳、休闲放松。

旅游是件美妙的事。但在以前,那似乎是很遥远的事。现在年轻人的生活方式与以前不同。事实证明旅游是缓解压力的好办法。众所周知,美国人喜欢旅游。美国年轻人只要有时间和旅费就会去旅游!这是与朋友分享的冒险。可以去落基山脉、夏威夷岛、佛罗里达州、德克萨斯州和纽约。这完全取决于你想做什么,爬山？冲浪？骑马？……这完全取决于你的兴趣和钱包。你有多少时间、多少钱？时间和金钱是两个主要问题,而这两个因素会决定你去哪里旅游、什么时间去,以及去多久。

许多美国中学生和大学生要去上学就必须打零工,甚至做全职工作。这意味着他们通常在下午、傍晚、周末和假期工作,以存足够的钱来支付学费以及购买书本、汽车和衣服。许多中产阶级的美国人无法为孩子支付所有的费用,因此他们的孩子就通过打工来贴补。因为这钱是用于读书而不是旅游的,只有当有多余的钱时(通常没有多少)才有机会到附近的地方去。旅游的时间是宝贵的;因此,如果一个学生只有两个星期,他/她必须要事先计划好,买便宜的票到能去得起的地方去。

作为年轻人,你们可以忍受没有很多食物、没有柔软的床、没有许多钱的生活。你们拥有健康,而健康就意味着力量、耐性和积极的人生观。你们很年轻,这让你们能自由地寻求冒险与享受这种感受!当你去旅游时,就是在打开一本书,其中每一页都是你生命中通往另一个领域的旅程。只要你愿意去接受这种经历……以及欢乐,就能从中获益!

有句谚语说,只是工作不会娱乐,使得杰克成为愚钝的人,这种观点你同意吗？在现代生活中,就象机器需要加燃料一样,人也需要时间去恢复充电。因为大脑和身体在工作一段时间后,必然会疲惫,就需要充分的休息。因此,有时为了更好地继续工作,我们应该停下来休息。另外,娱乐在很多方面对我们有益。玩是人的自然本能之一。除了学习和工作,玩耍、娱乐也能使人获得更多的生活体验。反过来,作为回报,这种体验可以应用于你的工作之中。

总而言之,作为现代人,我们应过现代的生活,努力工作,享受生活!

对话:中国新年

杨:鲍勃,新年快乐!

鲍勃:新年快乐!

杨:今天的天气真好!

鲍勃:这样的天气正适合新年呀。
杨:你打算怎样过年?
鲍勃:我想出去看看街道变为什么样了,人们的感觉如何。
杨:商店大都关门了,也许人们还在睡觉。除夕,中国人通常很忙碌,有些人玩通宵,早晨时都累了,就该睡觉啦。
鲍勃:除夕晚上,你们通常忙什么?
杨:看电视、喝酒、跳舞、唱歌、打牌、祭拜众神和祖先,这一切必须在清早前做完。
鲍勃:有什么特别的电视节目吗?
杨:有,中央电视台春节联欢晚会,海外华侨也能收看到这台特别节目。
鲍勃:你们去看望朋友吗?
杨:是的,但现在越来越少,有时,只是打个电话或发个短信问候一下,拜个年。
鲍勃:是这样啊。
杨:我们出去看看街上什么样了。
鲍勃:和昨天大不一样了。
杨:人们都喜气洋洋,忙着走亲访友。
鲍勃:看那家银行,装饰得真漂亮。
杨:我认为现在新年的装饰变得越来越精致。
鲍勃:没有那些装饰,就不像新年啦。
杨:是啊,撤下去,就感觉有点儿冷清。
鲍勃:那就提醒我们又过了一年。
杨:假期结束,我们也要精力充沛地重返工作岗位,有个新的开始。

第4单元 邮政局

Text A

邮政电信服务

在英国,邮局通常在周一至周五的上午八点半或九点到下午五点半或六点营业。大街上的邮筒都漆成红颜色。

邮政服务可以分为两个等级:一等和二等。前一种可以享受很多优待,但邮资较高。好处是邮递速度快。后一种往往要比前一种晚24小时。

如果愿意,你可以寄明信片。两种等级的服务都可以按照信的价格投递。一定记住千万不要以寄信方式寄包裹,那非常贵。你可以用包裹的邮寄方式来邮寄。这样很慢,但便宜得多。

  美国的邮政制度是从它作为英国殖民地时的邮政服务派生而成的。1847年第一次使用邮票(英国1839年开始使用)。19世纪由于人口西移,遥远的路途给邮政服务工作提出了快速投递的问题。那时,骑马快速投递为不同地方之间提供快速邮政服务。熟练的骑手轻装上阵,快马加鞭,接力传递。骑手要跑75~100英里到另一驿站,期间换马6~8次,休息一段时间后把邮件往回送。

  如今,美国的邮电服务是有竞争对手的。信使专递可以收发信函;许多公司也运送包裹和货物。通过邮局安全投递有两种方式:挂号邮件和保证邮件。保证邮件要便宜得多。你在任何城市都可以通过"存局候领"收到邮件。邮局将保留十天,如果发信人在信封上写上"请保留三十天",邮局将最多保留一个月。使用邮政编码能加快投递。

  电话在日常生活中提供了简单快捷的办事途径。一天中,你可能几次地通过电话询问旅游事宜。电话可以节省时间和金钱。如果你想询问时间表或核查价格,如果你想乘火车、汽车或飞机,你就可以打电话查出时间、价格和其他信息,以便进行预定。电话随时随地都可打。还有付费电话(或公用电话),你投币或插卡之后就可以打了,旅行时是很方便的。

  总体来说,要找到一部公用电话是非常容易的。公用电话经常安装在以下场所:公共汽车站、火车站、飞机场、商店、旅馆、饭店、加油站、许多街角以及大多数的写字楼。但是,请记住:通常你不能在美国邮局打电话。

对话

对话A:在邮局

1 甲:早上好。

乙:早上好。我想寄一些明信片和一封信到荷兰。请把邮资告诉我好吗?

甲:一张明信片一元钱,信的邮资取决于信的质量和邮寄的方式,平寄、挂号,还是特快专递?

乙:我想寄航空挂号信。

对话B:邮有回执的挂号信

甲:能为您做些什么?

乙:我想寄两封信到加拿大。请问邮资是多少?

甲:您要怎样邮寄? 平信还是挂号?

乙:我还没决定好,你给提个建议。

甲:邮的什么?

乙:一些重要的商务文件。

甲:我建议你用有回执的挂号方式邮寄。

乙:什么是有回执的挂号信?和普通的挂号信有什么不同?
甲:有回执的挂号信是指在信寄出之后,您会得到一份收据回单。
乙:那太好了,就按这种方式邮吧。
甲:您的地址是用铅笔写的,那样不行。
乙:很抱歉。那我用钢笔重写。那封信行吗?
甲:完全可以。

第5单元　酒店服务

Text A

旅馆服务

　　如今旅馆服务的主要趋势是高速便捷。客人希望在旅馆里找到他们所需要的一切。为了满足客人的需要,旅馆将想尽一切办法来尝试。有各种不同层次和种类的酒店。最高级的是豪华型的。最低层的只是提供住宿的地方。为了适应各种目的,有商业旅馆、汽车旅馆、度假旅馆、居住旅馆和会议旅馆。在不同级别和不同类型的旅馆中,提供的服务也各不相同。
　　一般来说,正规旅馆服务包括前厅服务、客房服务、餐饮服务、娱乐服务、商店服务、安全保安服务。
　　前厅处理预定、接待、咨询方面的问题。预定员的工作就是预定、取消、更正、写并寄发宾馆预定的确认信。由于通讯特别发达,提前预定可通过电话、电报或传真。然后宾馆通过回复的传真确认客人的预定,同样客人发来的传真也可以作为客人的预定确认。
　　通常在宾馆的前厅接待客人,在那里他们登记、取房门钥匙、邮寄、咨询、存放贵重物品和结账。它也被称做接待处,在那里提供接待服务。前厅工作人员作为宾馆的代表,在能否经营成功方面起着重要作用。
　　客房服务指客房服务员对客人的房间需要提供的服务。如收拾房间、整理床铺、分发客房部所提供的物品、收集和送交洗涤衣物等。
　　餐饮是一个宾馆必不可少的组成部分。它所提供餐饮的利润占五分之二至一半。在大宾馆里,餐厅是由烧烤、各种酒吧、自助餐厅和包间组成的。餐饮部的工作人员,特别是男女招待员、酒吧招待员在餐厅的成功经营方面起着极其重要的作用。优秀的招待员应热情微笑、礼貌周全、态度诚恳、高效率地为顾客服务。
　　娱乐服务是为客人的休闲娱乐所提供的。许多宾馆含有很多娱乐设施,如舞厅、礼堂、泳池或健身中心。也有现代化的立体声音响和照明设备供客人随音乐唱歌跳舞。客人也可以使用体育器材进行一些体育锻炼。

  大多数宾馆有商店,在那里你可以买一些生活必需品,如旅游用品、手工艺品、地方特产、食品饮料、快餐等。客人们对这种服务感到很满意,因为他们不必走远路去买他们所需要的物品。

  直到最近几年一些宾馆才认为有必要提供保安服务。许多大宾馆(特别是市区内的)设立保安部目前很有必要。保安人员不仅保护宾馆客人及他们的财物也保护宾馆的财产。

  不同种类的旅馆为不同种类的客户提供服务。商业旅馆为短暂停留住宿的人——很多是出差旅行的人提供服务。很多城市宾馆及各种汽车旅馆属于这一类。商业旅馆和汽车旅馆所提供的服务与那些旅馆类似。但是汽车旅馆与其他旅馆最显著的区别是它可以自由停放车辆。其他旅馆几乎不能为所有客人提供这项服务。

  度假旅馆位于度假区或景区,它借助自然环境迎合度假者和想休闲娱乐者的需要。会议旅馆的服务主要针对会议安排方面的交易。这种旅馆都以各种餐厅、宴会厅、会议室、会堂和展览厅为特征。有些旅馆一次会议可容纳多达 4 000 名宾客。

  居住旅馆迎合那些自己不想拥有房子,只是季节性,甚至长久租用住处人的需要。居住旅馆通常是一个公寓楼,提供客房服务、餐厅服务,可能还有鸡尾酒吧服务。餐饮部只是给居住者带来方便的小部门。

  随着旅馆业的发展,将会有更多复杂的部门提供更多的服务。旅馆的声誉是由给客人提供舒适的程度及各项服务所决定的。"信誉第一,顾客至上"这一座右铭是永远不会改变的。

对话:在旅馆办理住宿登记

对话 A

A:我可以帮忙么,先生?

B:我想办理住宿登记手续。我叫比尔·史密斯。青年旅行社的王小姐已为我预定了一个单人间。

A:让我查一查。哦,是的,您已预定了五楼的一个单人间。

B:那儿有浴室么?

A:当然有。

B:室内有电话么?

A:是的,我们所有的房间都有电话。

B:那么,你们供餐么?

A:哦,是的,我们有很好的餐厅。我们 6:00~9:00 供应早餐;11:00~1:00 供应午餐;5:00~10:00 供应晚餐。

B:好吧,我想在这儿住一周。
A:请填写这个登记卡好么?
B:好吧。
A:这是512房的钥匙,我找一名行李工将您的行李拿上楼。
B:多谢了。
A:不用谢,如您有什么需要的话,给接待处打电话。
B:好,谢谢您了。

对话B

客人:晚上好,我是518房的格林先生。
楼层服务员:晚上好,格林先生,您有什么事吗?
客:我明天早晨7:30要参加一个研讨会,恐怕那么早我起不来,我想要叫醒服务。
楼:好的,格林先生,您想让我们什么时候叫您?
客:我说不准会花多长时间到达锦江宾馆。在这儿很容易叫出租车吗?
楼:当然,任何时候大厅门前都能叫到出租车。通常只用大约20分钟就到达那个宾馆。
客:那样的话,请在5:30分叫醒我。那么我会有时间洗漱,吃早餐。
楼:5:30吗?好吧,那么我们将在5:30叫醒您。好,晚安,格林先生。
客:谢谢您,晚安。

第6单元 家外之家

Text A

家外之家

人们可以把家定义为能感受到温暖、舒适、方便的窝巢和港湾。高质量的宾馆服务也能为所有需要休息、就餐、就饮的宾客营造一种家外之家气氛。宾馆服务应突出体现便捷、舒适、友谊、好客和互助。

便捷指的是具有实际价值和完整服务项目的,有形的宾馆服务设施,它会使宾客感到就像住在自己的别墅一样。

舒适指的是具有诱人价值的宾馆设施的质量,它会使下榻宾馆的宾客感受到结合了美的享受。

安全是指宾馆所有的总体气氛和令人愉快的环境,使宾客充满舒心愉快,体验"家"的那种无忧无虑。

友谊可理解为宾馆工作人员所给予的热情、友好、体贴、微笑的感情服务。它会使宾客留恋东方人的真情和人与人之间的友谊。

殷勤好客包括宾馆工作人员所具备的礼貌周全，礼节表现的服务。在各项服务中，这一点体现了中国人礼让的优秀传统。

互助是指宾馆工作人员应互相协作快速提供服务，以宾客的需要作为自己的工作目标，同时按着一定的程序和标准为宾客提供各项服务。这样，宾客在宾馆的消费会报以综合美的价值的享受。

宾馆的三个主要部门对宾客拥有"家"的感觉意义重大。宾馆的前厅不仅是"商店的窗口"，而且是"中枢神经"。当宾客进入前厅时，他们最先接触前厅工作人员。如果他们能热情、周到、彬彬有礼地为宾客服务，他们就能给宾客留下好印象。永久的印象对实现宾馆工作目标意义重大。就是在这个部门决定着宾客的假日或生意的成败，实际上也关系到宾馆运作的成败。

为圆满地完成工作任务，前厅工作人员应待客有礼，技巧熟练地为宾客服务，妥善地处理宾客的投诉，有效地解决宾客的困难。只有这样才能使宾客放心，对其他的服务满意，真正体验到"家"的温暖。

客房部重点注意客房和公共区域的卫生，为宾客提供舒适满意的客房设施。宾馆客房的收入是宾馆运作成败的关键。当宾客走进明亮、干净的房间时，他们非常满意，感觉就像在家一样。在宾客进住宾馆期间，客房服务员应热情、主动、耐心、周到地工作。

越来越多的宾馆经营者逐渐意识到餐饮服务是宾馆运作中另一个重要因素。在很多大宾馆中，它带来的收入要比零售客房多。在宾馆的餐厅有各个不同的区域提供各种餐饮服务，有烧烤厅、各种酒吧、自助餐厅、咖啡屋及客房就餐服务、休息室餐饮服务、宴会服务。餐饮经营在整个系统中是与各个部门复杂地结合在一起的。餐饮部需要全体工作人员的协同工作。所以团体的凝聚力尤其重要。餐饮部的工作人员，特别是男女招待员、酒吧招待员，在营造愉快气氛中起着极其重要的作用，这也是宾馆出售的一项服务。高质量的服务取决于招待员和其他餐饮部工作人员热爱本职工作，熟悉自己的业务直至细节问题。与宾客的最初接触非常重要。一个优秀的招待员既能立即满足宾客的需要，又能满足餐厅的需要。热情的微笑和彬彬有礼、真诚高效的服务会将更多的宾客带回"家"。

现代宾馆的发展趋势是为了使宾客享受家一样的待遇。宾馆工作人员应全身心地投入到工作中。他们应像对待朋友亲戚一样对待宾客，并方方面面为他们考虑。这种情感服务的魅力会使很多宾客成为自愿的宣传员，这对宾馆的经营来说比任何广告的影响还大。将会有越来越多的宾客愿意回到这个"家外之家"。

对话

对话 A：通知离开宾馆

甲：我要在大约下午 1 点钟结帐。

乙：您能马上腾出您的房间吗？

甲：那么，如果我马上腾出房间的话，能把我的东西寄存在这儿吗？

乙：当然。

甲：不，我不能。我要忙到一点钟因为我要花一些时间打点行装。

乙：恐怕要收您半天的房费。

甲：什麼？还要收费？我一大早两点多一点儿才到的。

乙：您说的对。但是，早晨五点以前到宾馆，就等于是前一天晚上到的。

甲：在中午之前就得腾出来多奇怪！

对话 B：结帐

甲：您好，我是 427 房间的威廉姆克顿。我想结帐。

乙：请等一下。我要写出您的帐单。您的帐单总数是 350 美元。

甲：让我看一下。好，这是 400 美元。

乙：这是您的 50 元零钱。感谢您的光临。希望再次见到您。

甲：谢谢。请开两张收据，因为餐饮是由我自己付费，住宿费是由公司付。

乙：请等一下。

甲：对不起，克顿先生。我让您久等了。请在收据上签上您的名字。

第 7 单元　中国美食

Text A

中国菜

中国菜以其美妙的味道和精致的技艺闻名世界。现在人们普遍认为它可以分成八大地方菜，尽管还有其他很多著名的地方菜，比如北京菜和上海菜。

山东菜

山东菜由济南菜和胶东菜组成，味道清爽、纯正、不油腻，以强调香、鲜、脆、嫩为主要特点。山东菜常用大葱和大蒜作调料。主要烹调技艺包括爆、熘、扒、烤、煮、蜜。

特色菜有：葱烧海参、糖醋黄河鲤鱼、生焖鲍鱼。

四川菜

四川菜是一种很著名的中国菜。以辛辣、刺激的口味为主要特点,四川菜口味多样,主要强调使用辣椒和花椒粉。烹饪时也会用蒜、姜、豆豉等调料。食用草药、家禽、鸟常用作做菜的原料。烹饪技艺有嫩煎、爆、干煸、脆等。

特色菜有:宫保鸡丁、回锅肉、麻婆豆腐。

广东菜

广东菜由广州菜、潮州菜和东江菜组成,以选料新鲜、口味鲜嫩著称。广东菜的主要原料有:海鲜、淡水鱼和家禽等。基本烹调技艺有:烤、炒、嫩煎、炸、焖、炖和蒸。最常使用蒸和炒来保持原料的原味。广东厨师也很注重菜式的精美雅致。

特色菜有:鱼翅汤、脆皮乳鸽、蚝油牛肉。

福建菜

福建菜由福州菜、泉州菜、厦门菜组成,以其海鲜选料、色美、腌制口味著称。

特色菜有:佛跳墙和龙身凤尾虾。

湖南菜

湖南菜由湘江菜、洞庭湖地区菜、和湘西地区菜组成。其特色是口味浓重、辛辣。辣椒、胡椒和葱在湖南菜中通常是必不可少的。

特色菜有:东安子鸡、麻辣童子鸡和蒸蜡肉。

淮阳菜

淮阳菜也叫江苏菜,主要由江南水乡的扬州、镇江、和淮安菜组成。它不仅选料精良,而且以刀工精细、造型美观、制作精美、赏心悦目而闻名。烹调技艺包括:炖、焖、烤和煨。淮阳菜口味清淡、鲜嫩、味甜,而且菜式精美雅致。

特色菜有:松鼠鳜鱼、水晶肉、脆皮鳝鱼。

浙江菜

浙江菜由杭州、宁波和绍兴等地方菜组成,以其鲜、嫩、软、滑的香醇口味而著称。杭州菜是其中最著名的。

特色菜有:西湖醋鱼、龙井虾仁、叫化鸡。

安徽菜

安徽菜特别注重烹调温度,安徽厨师擅长焖和炖。常加入火腿提味,加入冰糖提鲜。

特色菜有:茶叶熏鸡和黄山炖鸽。

对话

对话 A:定一间八人雅间

服务员:这里是春天饭店。早上好,您要帮忙吗?

客人:我要定一间八人雅间,今晚用。

服务员:当然可以。您什么时候到?

客人:大约7点钟。

服务员:可以留一下姓名吗,先生?

客人:就以怀特先生的名义定餐吧。你能告诉我房间名吗?

服务员:我们为您安排"彩虹"间吧。您现在点菜吗?

客人:不点,我们晚上点。

服务员:您还要我们准备什么吗?

客人:不用了。谢谢。

服务员:不客气。再见。

客人:再见。

对话 B:点牛排

服务员:可以请您点菜了吗,先生?

客人:是的,我要一份牛排。

服务员:您的牛排要做到什么火候的?嫩的、半熟的还是熟透的?

客人:我要嫩的。

服务员:您的牛排要配什么菜啊?

客人:豌豆和胡萝卜。

服务员:您要土豆泥、烤土豆还是煮土豆?

客人:请给我一份烤土豆。

服务员:您要不要来份沙拉,先生?

客人:好的,你能给推荐一下吗?

服务员:什锦蔬菜沙拉或是番茄沙拉怎么样?

客人:我要一份番茄沙拉。

第8单元　中国茶

Text A

中国茶

中国是茶叶的故乡。中国人种植茶叶的历史可以追溯到战国时期。一千多年以前,茶叶作为出口商品已经闻名世界。人们认为 tea 这个词来源于中国字"茶"。尽管英语单词 tea 的发音与普通话"茶"(cha)的发音不一样,但是它的发音与厦门方言"茶"的发音相似。

茶叶的种类

按照不同的生产工艺,中国茶可分为五种:绿茶、红茶、乌龙茶、压缩茶(砖茶)和茉莉花茶。

绿茶在生产工艺中不用发酵,保持了茶叶原来的颜色。它主要包括:浙江龙井、安徽黄山毛峰和江苏碧螺春。

红茶在烘干之前需要发酵。最好的红茶品牌有安徽祁红、云南滇红、江苏苏红、四川川红和湖南湘红。

乌龙茶的工艺介于绿茶和红茶之间,是经过部分发酵后生产出来的。它是中国东南沿海地区的特产,包括:福建、广东和台湾。

压缩茶易于运输和贮藏,主要供往偏远地区。大多数的压缩茶都制成砖形,因此,一般被称为"砖茶",尽管有些时候也被制成蛋糕和碗的形状。压缩茶主要产于湖北、湖南、四川和云南。

茉莉花茶是干的茶叶和茉莉花混合而成的。深受中国北方人和越来越多的外国人的喜爱。

喝茶的好处

中国人喜欢饭后饮一杯茶,而且通常会用茶招待客人。茶叶是中国人日常生活的必需品之一。

而且,喝茶有助于保持健康。茶叶有助于分解脂肪和促进消化。因此,对于许多主要以肉食为生的中国少数民族来说特别重要。他们有一句流行的谚语:"宁可三日无盐,不可一日无茶。"

茶叶富含多种维生素。它有助于吸烟的人把尼古丁排出体外。据说茶叶还能帮助醉酒的人醒酒。

然而,这并不意味着茶越浓益处就越多。据报道,经常饮用过浓的茶水对有些人来说会导致心脏和血压紊乱,而且会使年轻人的牙齿变黑。

最后,我们还得记住,一定不要用滚开的水泡茶,因为那样会破坏茶叶中的维生素。最合适的水温应该不超过80℃。

对话

对话 A:在酒吧

服务员:晚上好!您想喝点什么吗?

杰克:是的。但是请给我们几分钟先看看饮料单。

服务员:好的。

杰克:我们看一下……鸡尾酒、白兰地、雪利酒、利口酒、苏格兰威士忌……这里是啤酒。我要五星啤酒。苏珊,你呢?

苏珊:我要香格里。

杰克:香格里是什么?

苏珊:是一种由红葡萄酒、柠檬汁、橙汁和糖调制的鸡尾酒。

杰克:听起来不错。好的,服务员,给我来一份五星啤酒,给她一份香格里。

服务员:一份五星啤酒和一份香格里。谢谢。

对话 B:抱怨点餐上迟了

客人:服务员,我点的饮料呢?怎么回事?我们已经等了20分钟了,可是饮料还没上。

服务员:对不起,先生。我去找送酒员问问。

客人:那么,请快点,我们不能再等下去了。

服务员:我马上回来。

……

服务员:很抱歉让您久等了。您点的饮料马上到。

客人:好的。

送酒员:这是您点的饮料。实在抱歉,上晚了,耽误了您的时间。请享用您的饮料。

第9单元　观光

Text A

人们旅游的原因

旅游业的增长已经成为当代全世界各个国家的共同现象。据世界贸易组织预计,只出境游客一项就由1994年的54.6亿增长到2010年的93.7亿。但人们为什么这样喜欢旅游?

据马斯洛讲,在每个人的普遍需求中都存在着等级。最低级的就是对生存的需要。最高级的需要是对自我实现、本人才能的充分发挥的需要,也就是对提高自身潜力、美学的激励的需要及对创建自我个性等的需要。当个人的生存需要得到满足后,人们很自然地会去寻求对其他需求的满足。旅游就成了一个很好的选择,因为它提供了大量满足人们需要的机会,转而,又构成人们旅游和度假的主要动力因素。

可能旅游最常见的原因和我们的身体健康有关。实际上,为了运动而旅游成了增长最快的原因之一。然而,可供观赏的运动的动力是更为复杂的。人们有摆脱常规的欲望,和团体保持一致,这样会给他们带来归属感,向往如果他参与而能完成的角色。这一点,精神上的影响要大于身体上的影响。在快速发展的现代社会,紧张和压力成为个人生活的一部分,人们想通过改变环境和活动来休息和放松。

另一个重要的动力因素和文化、好奇心有关,这可以从想了解其他地区、国家,寻求不同体验的欲望中看出。没有人怀疑旅游能开阔视野。大旅游发展的原因正是由求知欲引起的。现今,这种欲望正由像电视、飞机这样的现代媒体所助长,来游遍世界的每个角落。当一个人游览过一个特别的地方,他会更加关注新闻、电视节目对它的报道。通过了解其他文化,一个人也能发展自身的文化,从而真正丰富自己的思想。

归属感的需要从对拜访亲友,结交新的朋友的欲望中得到体现。人都是社会的人,需要和他人接触交流。在旅游中,有这种目的的人更注重旅游的过程而不是目的地。当然,如果亲朋住在奇异有趣的地方也能促进旅游的发生。为了迎合这一需要,许多旅行社专门推出了重返故乡寻根的旅游路线。

当人们为了提高专业知识而去外地开会,这时,他们更关注自身的提高。这增强了他们的自尊。人们也从他人那里寻求自尊。据说,在旅游业中存在"随大溜"的说法。也就是指,一些人去过一些地方,而另一些人也想去像那些人一样去同样的地方。作为第一个去某个奇异的地方,或去某个特殊的地方的人,确实能让人兴奋,并让朋友羡慕。

需要和欲望的结合确实给现今最大的产业之一——旅游业带来原动力,然而,人们去旅游不仅需要动力。在一个人认真计划一次旅游之前,还有两个因素是非常重要的:空闲时间和无条件收益(个人收入中减去了必需支出)。

空闲时间可以定义为必要劳动后的自由时间。空闲的两个方面对促进旅游业是很重要的:可能的空闲时间和对空闲时间的态度。自二战后,个人的空闲时间普遍增加了。一周的工作时间从60小时减少到40小时,工作时间的减少仍在发达国家和发展中国家继续。另外,为了改变社会状况,已经把休闲时间作为一种生活方式,休闲就成了社会中无可非议的一个方面。增加的空闲时间开始被用在消遣娱乐活动上而不是工作上。

无条件收益或可任意使用的工资,是不必用在个人必需的吃、穿、健康、交通等上的钱。家庭规模的变小和劳动力市场上女性数量的增加使得今天的家庭更富裕,从而大大促进了旅游业。

运输业的发展在很大程度上促进了旅游的发展。在大规模以火车、汽车为交通工具后,是以飞机为交通工具的发展。今天,在许多国家,建立了公路系统以便让人们在不同的城市,甚至不同国家间的旅游不会在公路上受到一个红灯的影响,也不会在同一条公路上受到双行交通的影响。庞大的公路系统、航空连接、人们可以负担得起的汽车的大量生产,这些都使得旅游产业达到了历史上从未有过的发展速度。随着人们生活水平的提高、空闲时间的增加,及旅游花费的相对降低,旅游业必将持续发展。

对话

对话 A

A: 早上好,夫人。

B: 早上好。我想用今天一天的时间来游览。你能建议一下我去什么样的地方好?

A: 当然。早晨去 Bund 怎么样?你会看到许多人在那晨练、跳扇子舞、拳击等。

B: 那一定很有趣。

A: 确实如此。然后去 Yu 花园,那很好找。它是上海最著名的景点之一,值得一游。顺便你可以在那里的茶馆品尝典型的中国茶。

B: 真是个好主意。

A: 下午你最好去黄浦江——上海的母亲河,在亚洲最高的电视塔——东方明珠电视塔上鸟瞰整个上海。

B: 太棒了。

对话 B

A: 这是我第一次来英国,你能为我提点建议吗?

B: 你在这儿的时间长吗?

A: 仅仅五天出差时间。

B: 这里有很多旅游景点。你真该去看看格林尼治公园。你去过那儿吗?

A: 没去过,我打算明天去。

B: 我有一些关于旅游方面的资料,你想看看吗?

A: 你真是太好了。

A: 给你。

第 10 单元 旅游购物

Text A

旅游商品

旅游商品是游客在旅程中购买的有形的商品。由大量手工艺术品、文化纪念品及仿制品、土特产、旅游纪念品、游客每天必需的商品和其他各种日常用品构成。

旅游商品显示了与一般商品的不同。从生产和经营的角度看,一般商品主要为大众服务,满足他们的日常需要,而旅游商品一般为游客服务。换句话说,旅游商品被认为是旅游目的地生产经营的为满足国内外游客在此旅游的需要的物质产品。

对于消费者和商品的关系,游客对旅游商品的期望和居民对一般商品的期望有所不同。前者对商品的花色、品种、质量、等级、样式、包装和装饰的选择比后者有更高、更特殊的需要。游客特别看重旅游商品的纪念性、艺术价值和实用性。纪念性是旅游商品非常重要的一面。它能够显示旅游目的地特点,旅游的时间,作为游客参加某个旅游活动的证明,从而在将来给游客带来对此次旅游的回忆。艺术性指旅游商品的新奇性和精美的设计,能给人以美的享受,并赋予了情感价值。实用性,说明旅游商品对游客有实际的使用价值。例如,旅游商品除了要耐用外,还需要轻便、多功能和变携。

此外,旅游商品的销售在陈列、摊位布局上有其自身的特点。由于旅游商品主要服务于游客这一特点,其交易和摊位的安排也和主要满足当地居民的一般商品不同。卖一般商品的商店为了方便居民通常建在居民区,通常分布得很好。经营旅游商品的商店通常建在旅游城市的商业繁华区,靠近风景名胜区、旅店和购物中心的地方。这一布局是由旅游活动的特殊特点引起。许多商家在机场、码头、车站的出入口向外国游客出售旅游商品。外国游客在离开前可以在免税商店购买旅游商品,这是国际惯例。免税商店多数经营烟草、酒类商品。另外,他们也零售其他高级商品。由于这些商品免除了进口税而且价格低,对游客来说是廉价货。

最后,旅游商品和一般商品在生产和经营的波动上也不同。游客的数量对旅游商品的生产和销售有直接的影响。旅游潮流受到如经济、政治、自然环境、社会环境等各类因素的影响。另外,游客不像固定居民那样,他们是流动的群体。由于随着时间、地点的不同和游客流动的变化,旅游商品的生产和销售的波动也很大。

对话

对话 A

A：请问什么地方卖女鞋？

B：在三楼，夫人。

A：谢谢，我还想知道你们店里有没有快餐厅？

B：有，在五楼。

A：有电梯吗？

B：有，请乘六号电梯，夫人。

A：非常感谢你。

B：不必客气。

对话 B

A：对不起，打扰一下，您在挑选商品时请不要乱放。

B：哦，非常抱歉，我找不到我要买的那种糖果了。

A：也许目前缺货，何不换别的牌子试试呢？

B：我拿不准别的糖果是否和我要买的那种一样好。

A：您尽可放心，实际上，我们这里出售的所有商品的质量都是有保证的。

B：那么，我就试试看。

APPENDIX 3
Glossary

词 汇 表

A

as well as	也，又
air hostess	空姐
attention to	对……注意
abalone /ˌæbəˈləuni/	n. 鲍鱼
accessible /əkˈsesibəl/	adj. 容易获得的
accommodate /əˈkɔmədeit/	vt. 容纳，供应
accommodation /əˌkɔməˈdeiʃən/	n. 膳宿供应
acknowledgement /əkˈnɔlidʒmənt/	n. 承认
actualization /ˌæktʃuəlaiˈzeiʃən/	n. 现实，现实化
adept /əˈdept/	adj. 内行的，熟练的
adopt /əˈdɔpt/	v. 采用，采纳
advantage /ədˈvɑːntidʒ/	n. 利益、优点、长处
adventure /ədˈventʃə/	n. 冒险
aesthetic /iːsˈθetik/	adj. 美的，艺术的
affluence /ˈæfluəns/	n. 丰富，富裕
affluent /ˈæfluənt/	adj. 富裕的，丰富的
affordable /əˈfɔːdəbl/	adj. 能负担得起的
agent /ˈeidʒənt/	n. 代理人，代理商
Amoy /əˈmɔi/	n. 厦门方言
ample /ˈæmpəl/	adj. 足够的
announcement /əˈnaunsmənt/	n. 宣告，发表
anxious /ˈæŋkʃəs/	adj. 渴望的
applicability /ˌæplikəˈbiliti/	n. 适用性
aroma /əˈrəumə/	n. 香味，芳香，香气
aspect /ˈæspekt/	n. 方面
assortment /əˈsɔːtmənt/	n. 花色品种
assure /əˈʃuə/	v. 保证
atmosphere /ˈætməsfiə/	n. 气氛

attachment	/əˈtætʃmənt/	n. 依恋，附属品
attribute	/əˈtribju:t/	n./vt. 归因，属性
auditorium	/ˌɔ:diˈtɔ:riəm/	n. 礼堂
available	/əˈveiləbl/	adj. 可得到的，可利用的，有空的

B

be tired of		厌烦
by no means		决不
baggage	/ˈbægidʒ/	n. 行李
banquet	/ˈbæŋkwit/	n. 宴会
bargain	/ˈbɑ:gin/	n. 廉价货
bartender	/ˈbɑ:ˌtendə/	n. 酒吧间招待员
benefit	/ˈbenifit/	v. (因……)得到利益
beverage	/ˈbevəridʒ/	n. 饮料
braise	/breiz/	vt. (用文火)焖
briefing	/ˈbri:fiŋ/	n. 情况介绍，简报
burden	/ˈbə:dən/	n. 负担

C

consist of		由……组成
cabin	/ˈkæbin/	n. 小屋，机舱
cafeteria	/ˌkæfiˈtiəriə/	n. 自助食堂
cancel	/ˈkænsəl/	v. 取消
cancellation	/ˌkænsəˈleiʃən/	n. 取消，撤消
cargo	/ˈkɑ:gəu/	n. 货物
cater	/ˈkeitə/	vi. 迎合，投合
catering	/ˈkeitəriŋ/	n. 公共饮食业；给养
ceiling	/ˈsi:liŋ/	n. 天花板
certify	/ˈsə:tifai/	v. 保证
challenge	/ˈtʃælindʒ/	n. 挑战
chamber	/ˈtʃeimbə/	n. 房间，寝室
chambermaid	/ˈtʃeimbəmeid/	n. 女服务员
characterize	/ˈkæriktəraiz/	vt. 具有……的特征/特性/特色
charm	/tʃɑ:m/	n. 魅力
check	/tʃek/	v. 检查
cheerful	/ˈtʃiəful/	adj. 快活的，愉快的
chef	/ʃef/	n. 厨师，主厨，大师傅

citizen	/ˈsitizən/	n. 市民，公民
citizenship	/ˈsitizənʃip/	n. 公民身份
classify	/ˈklæsifai/	vt. 把……分类
clientele	/ˌkli:ənˈtel/	n. 委托人，顾客
cockpit	/ˈkɔkpit/	n. 驾驶员座舱
cohesiveness	/kəuˈhi:sivnis/	n. 粘和，紧密结合在一起
colonial	/kəˈləuniəl/	adj. 殖民地的
combine	/kəmˈbain/	vt. 使结合
comfort	/ˈkʌmfət/	n. 舒适
comity	/ˈkɔmiti/	n. 礼让
commemorative	/kəˈmemərətiv/	adj. 纪念的
commercial	/kəˈmə:ʃəl/	adj. 商业的
commodity	/kəˈmɔdəti/	n. 商品
competitor	/kəmˈpetitə/	n. 竞争者
complaint	/kəmˈpleint/	n. 抱怨，投诉
complex	/ˈkɔmpleks/	adj. 复杂的
component	/kəmˈpəunənt/	n. 组成部分
comprehensive	/ˌkɔmpriˈhensiv/	adj. 综合的
compress	/kəmˈpres/	vt. 压缩，紧压
concerning	/kənˈsɔ:niŋ/	prep. 关于
confirmation	/ˌkɔnfəˈmeiʃən/	n. 确定，核实
confiscate	/ˈkɔnfiskeit/	v. 没收
consult	/kənˈsʌlt/	v. 查询
content	/ˈkɔntent/	n. 内容
convenience	/kənˈvi:niəns/	n. 方便
cordial	/ˈkɔ:diəl/	adj. 热诚的，亲切的
coteau	/kəuˈtəu/	n. 丘陵地，高地
courier	/ˈkuriə/	n.（递送重要文件的）信差
courtesy	/ˈkə:tisi/	n. 礼貌，殷勤
crew	/kru:/	n. 全体人员
crystallize	/ˈkristəlaiz/	vt. 1. 将(水果)浸糖 2. 使……结晶
cuisine	/kwiˈzi:n/	n. 烹调(法)
curiosity	/ˌkjuəriˈɔsiti/	n. 好奇心
customs	/ˈkʌstəmz/	n. 海关

D

draw up		写出,草拟
duty-free		adj.免税的
decoration	/ˌdekəˈreiʃən/	n.装饰
decrease	/ˈdiːkriːs/	v.使减少
deluxe	/diˈlʌks/	adj.豪华的,奢华的
demonstration	/ˌdemənˈstreiʃən/	n.示范
departure	/diˈpɑːtʃə/	n.启程,离开
deplane	/ˌdiˈplein/	v.下飞机
deposit	/diˈpɔzit/	v.放置
derive	/diˈraiv/	v.起源
destination	/ˌdestiˈneiʃən/	n.(旅行的)目的地,终点
determine	/diˈtəːmin/	v.决心,决定
digestion	/diˈdʒestʃən/	n.消化,消化作用
direct	/diˈrekt/	v.指引,指向
discharge	/disˈtʃɑːdʒ/	vt. 1.排放,排出,流出 2.释放,解雇
disembark	/ˌdisimˈbɑːk/	v.(使)起岸,(使)登陆
diversely	/daiˈvəːsli/	adv.多样地,多变化地
divide	/diˈvaid/	v.把……分成……
document	/ˈdɔkjumənt/	n.文件,文献
downtown	/ˈdaunˈtaun/	n.市中心
dual	/ˈdjuːəl/	adj.二重的
dynamic	/daiˈnæmik/	adj.有力的,有生气的

E

ease	/iːz/	n.舒适,安逸,自在
economy	/iˈkɔnəmi/	n.经济,节约,经济舱
edible	/ˈedibl/	adj.可食的,食用的
efficient	/iˈfiʃənt/	adj.有效的
efficiently	/iˈfiʃəntli/	adv.有效地
elaborate	/iˈlæbərət/	adj.精致的,精心的
embody	/imˈbɔdi/	vt.体现
emergency	/iˈməːdʒənsi/	n.紧急情况,突然事件
employee	/implɔiˈiː/ & /emplɔiˈiː/	n.雇员
endow	/inˈdau/	vt.赋予
endurance	/inˈdjuərəns/	n.忍耐,耐久力

energetic	/ˌenəˈdʒetik/	adj.精力充沛的
enthusiasm	/inˈθjuːziæzəm/	n.热情
enviable	/ˈenviəbl/	adj.值得羡慕的
equipment	/iˈkwipmənt/	n.装备,器材
escape	/iˈskeip/	v.逃脱
especially	/iˈspeʃəli/	adv.特别,尤其
establish	/iˈstæbliʃ/	v.建立,设立
esteem	/iˈstiːm/	vt/n.尊重,尊敬
esthetic	/ˌiːsˈθetik/ & /ˌesˈθetik/	adj.审美的
ethnic	/ˈeθnik/	adj.种族的,人种学的
etiquette	/ˈetiket/	n.礼节,礼仪
exempt	/igˈzempt/	vt.使免除
exhibit	/igˈzibit/	vt.表现
exotic	/igˈzɔtik/	adj.外国的,奇异的

F

fill out		填写
first class		一流的,头等舱
facilitate	/fəˈsiliteit/	vt.便利,促进
facility	/fəˈsiləti/	n.设备,工具
favorite	/ˈfeivərit/	adj.心爱的,最喜爱的
feature	/ˈfiːtʃə/	vt.以……为特色
ferment	/fəˈment/	vi/vt.发酵
fermentation	/fəːmenˈteiʃn/	n.发酵
fistulous onion	/ˈfistjuləsˈʌniən/	n.大葱
flavor	/ˈfleivə/	n.(独特的)味道,(包括不同味道的)风味
fledgling	/ˈfledʒliŋ/	n.刚长毛的(刚会飞的)雏鸟
fluctuate	/ˈflʌktjueit/	v.波动
foremost	/ˈfɔːməust/	adj.最重要的,最先的
fowl	/faul/	n.家禽,鸡肉,鸟肉
freight	/freit/	n.货物,(货物)运输
function	/ˈfʌŋkʃn/	n.功能,作用
furthermore	/ˈfəːðəˈmɔː/	adv.此外

G

garlic	/ˈgɑːlik/	n.大蒜
genealogical	/ˌdʒiːniəˈlɔdʒikəl/	adj.家谱的,家系的

generation	/ˌdʒenəˈreiʃn/	n. 同时代的人们，一代
geographic	/ˌdʒi:əuˈgræfik/	adj. 地理学的，地理的
ginger	/ˈdʒindʒə/	n. 姜
greasy	/ˈgri:si/	adj. 油腻的，脂肪多的
grill	/ˈgril/	n. 烤架，烧烤

H

hang on		不挂断，稍等
hallway	/ˈhɔ:lwei/	n. 走廊
handicraft	/ˈhændikra:ft/	n. 工艺品
herb	/hə:b/	n. 草，药草
hierarchy	/ˈhaiəra:ki/	n. 等级制度；体系，门类
hospitality	/ˌhɔspiˈtæliti/	n. 好客，殷勤
hotelier	/həuˈteliei/	n. 旅馆老板

I

in terms of		根据，按照，用……的话，在……方面
in the case of		在……的情况
identification	/aiˌdentifiˈkeiʃn/	n. 身份证明，识别
illusion	/iˈlu:ʒn/	n. 幻觉，幻影
imitation	/ˌimiˈteiʃn/	n. 仿制品
immigrate	/ˈimiˈgrənt/	v. 使移居入境，移来
immigration	/ˌimiˈgreiʃn/	n. 外来的移民，移居入境
implication	/ˌimpliˈkeiʃn/	n. 含义，暗示
impression	/imˈpreʃn/	n. 印象
indicate	/ˈindikeit/	vt. 显示，说明
indispensable	/ˌindiˈspensəbl/	adj. 必不可少的
individual	/ˌindiˈvidʒuəl/	n. 个人
inevitably	/inˈevitəbl/	adv. 不可避免地
infallibly	/inˈfæləbli/	adv. 没有错误地，确实可靠地
influence	/ˈinfluəns/	n./v. 影响
ingredient	/inˈgri:diənt/	n. 成分，原料，材料
initiative	/iˈniʃətiv/	n. 主动性
intend	/inˈtend/	v. 想要，打算
intention	/inˈtenʃn/	n. 意图，目的
involve	/inˈvɔlv/	v. 卷入
issue	/ˈiʃu:/	v. 发放，发行

J

jasmine	/ˈdʒæsmin/	n. 茉莉
justifiable	/ˈdʒʌstifaiəbl/	adj. 正当的,有理的

K

keep track of	明了

L

layout	/ˈleiaut/	n. 设计,布局
leisure	/ˈleʒə/	n. 空闲,闲暇
length	/leŋθ/	n. 长度
level	/ˈlevəl/	n. 水平
locate	/ləuˈkeit/	v. 确定……的位置
loudspeaker	/ˌlaudˈspiːkə/	n. 扬声器
lounge	/laundʒ/	n. 休息处,休息室
luxury	/ˈlʌkʃəri/	n. 奢侈,奢侈品

M

magnificent	/mæɡˈnifisnt/	adj.(建筑物、景色等)雄伟的、壮丽的
mainly	/ˈmeinli/	adv. 大体上,主要地
major	/ˈmeidʒə/	adj. 主要的
manifest	/ˈmænifest/	vt. 证明,显示
mechanic	/miˈkænik/	n. 机械工,技工
mellow	/ˈmeləu/	adj. 甜而多汁的,芳醇的
merchandise	/ˈməːtʃəndaiz/	n. 商品
minority	/maiˈnɔriti/	n. 少数,少数派,少数民族
miscellaneous	/ˌmisiˈleinjəs/	adj. 各种的
moreover	/mɔːˈrəuvə/	adv. 并且,除此之外
motivational	/ˌməutiˈveiʃənl/	adj. 动力的,有动机的
motto	/ˈmɔtəu/	n. 格言,箴言
mutual aid	/ˈmjuːtjuəlˈeid/	相互帮助
myriad	/ˈmiriəd/	n. 无数,众多

N

necessity	/niˈsesiti/	n. 必要的东西,必须品
nerve	/nəːv/	n. 神经
nicotine	/ˈnikətiːn/	n. 尼古丁
normally	/ˈnɔːməli/	adv. 通常,一般地
novelty	/ˈnɔːvəlti/	n. 新奇的东西

O

offer	/ˈɔfə/	vt.提供
opinion	/əˈpinjən/	n.观点
ordinary	/ˈɔːdinəri/	adj.普通的
organization	/ˌɔːgənaiˈzeiʃən/	n.组织,机构
originate	/əˈridʒineit/	v.开始,创造出,产生出
outlook	/ˈautluk/	n.展望,见解

P

play an important role in		在……中起重要作用
pace	/peis/	n.步速,速度,步态
package	/ˈpækidʒ/	n.包裹,包
parcel	/ˈpaːsəl/	n.包裹
partial	/ˈpaːʃəl/	adj.部分的,局部的,不完全的
perform	/pəˈfɔːm/	v.履行,执行
permanent	/ˈpəːmənənt/	adj.永久的
permanently	/ˈpəːmənəntli/	adv.永久地
permission	/pəˈmiʃən/	n.许可
personnel	/ˌpəːsəˈnel/	n.人员,员工
phenomenon	/fiˈnɔminən/	n.现象
photography	/fəˈtɔgrəfi/	n.摄影术;照相术
pillar	/ˈpilə/	n.柱状物
pillar-box	/ˈpiləˈbɔks/	n.圆柱状的邮筒
positive	/ˈpɔzətiv/	adj.积极的
prawn	/prɔːn/	n.对虾
pray	/prei/	v.祈祷
prefer	/priˈfəː/	v.更喜欢,宁愿
priority	/praiˈɔriti/	n.优先(权)
procedure	/prəuˈsiːdʒə/	n.程序,手续
profit	/ˈprɔfit/	n.利润
promise	/ˈprɔmis/	v./n.许诺,答应
propagandist	/ˌprɔpəˈgændist/	n.宣传员
proverb	/ˈprɔvəːb/	n.谚语,格言
pungent	/ˈpʌndʒənt/	adj.味道刺激性强的,辛辣的,刺鼻的
purpose	/ˈpəːpəs/	n.目的,意图
purser	/ˈpəːsə/	n.事务长

R

receipt	/ri'si:t/	n.收据
reception	/ri'sepʃn/	n.接待,接受
recommend	/ˌrekə'mend/	v.推荐,介绍
recreation	/ˌrekri'eiʃən/	n.娱乐、消遣
register	/'redʒistə/	vt.登记
registered	/'redʒistəd/	adj.挂号的
relic	/'relik/	n.纪念物,遗迹
relieve	/ri'li:v/	v.解除,减轻
remind	/ri'maind/	v.提醒
reply	/ri'plai/	vt.回复,答复
represent	/'repri'zent/	v.代表
representative	/ˌrepri'zentətiv/	n.代理,代表
reputation	/ˌrepju'teiʃən/	n.名誉,声望
reservation	/ˌrezə'veiʃən/	n.订购,预约
reservationist	/ˌrezə'veiʃənist/	n.预定员
resident	/'rezidənt/	n.居民
residential	/ˌrezi'denʃəl/	adj.居住的
resolve	/ri'zɒlv/	vt.分解,下决心,决定,解决
resort	/ri'zɔ:t/	n.胜地,度假之地
response	/ri'spɒns/	n.回应,反应
retail	/'ri:teil/	n.零售
revision	/ri'viʒn/	n.修正,校订
rewarding	/ri'wɔ:diŋ/	adj.报答的,有益的,值得的

S

seat belt		座椅安全带
sign in		签到,记录到达时间,签收
sanitation	/ˌsæni'teiʃən/	n.卫生
saute	/'səutei/	adj.嫩煎的
scenery	/'si:nəri/	n.景色,风景
schedule	/'ʃedju:l/	n.日程表
section	/'sekʃn/	n.部分,区
security	/si'kjuəriti/	n.安全
seminar	/'semina:/	n.研讨会
sensibility	/ˌsensi'biliti/	n.情感,感情,敏感

sentimental	/ˌsentiˈmentəl/	adj.感伤的,多愁善感的
separate	/ˈsepəreit/	adj.单独的
shallot	/ʃəˈlɒt/	n.冬葱,青葱
shelled	/ˈʃeld/	adj.脱壳的,去壳的
sign	/sain/	n.标记,符号
simmer	/ˈsimə/	v.煨
skiing	/ˈskiːiŋ/	n.滑雪
sober	/ˈsəubə/	vt/vi 变冷静,变严肃
somewhat	/ˈsʌmhwɒt/	adv.稍微,有点
source	/sɔːs/	n.源头,根源
souvenir	/ˈsuːvəniə/	n.纪念品
soybean	/ˈsɔibiːn/	n.大豆
special	/ˈspeʃəl/	adj.特别的
spicy	/ˈspaisi/	adj.辛辣的,芳香的,加有香料的
stereo	/ˈsteriəu/	n.立体声
stew	/stjuː/	vt.以文火煮,炖,烩
stick	/stik/	(stuck,stuck)v.固定,粘住
stimulating	/ˈstimjuleitiŋ/	adj.刺激的,有刺激性的
strain	/strein/	n.紧张,负担
sufficient	/səˈfiʃənt/	adj.充分的
suit	/sjuːt/	n.一套衣服
surf	/sɔːf/	v.参加冲浪运动

T

tangible	/ˈtændʒəbl/	adj.可触摸的
technique	/tekˈniːk/	n.技艺,技巧,技术
telegraph	/ˈteligrɑːf/	n.电报
telex	/ˈteleks/	n.用户电报
terminal	/ˈtəːminəl/	n.终点站,终端 adj.末期
territory	/ˈteritəri/	n.领域,范围
trace	/treis/	vt.追溯,追踪
transient	/ˈtrænziənt/	adj.短暂的,路过的
transmit	/trænzˈmit/	v.寄送
trend	/trend/	n.趋势
tuition	/tjuːˈiʃn/	n.(大学、书院等的)学费
type	/taip/	n.类型

U

ultimately	/ˈʌltimətli/	adv. 最终地，极限地

V

vacate	/vəˈkeit/	vt. 腾出，空出
valuable	/ˈvæljuəbl/	n. 贵重物品
villa	/ˈvilə/	n. 别墅
vinegar	/ˈvinigə/	n. 醋
visible	/ˈvizəbl/	adj. 看得见的
vitamin	/ˈvitəmin/	n. 维生素，维他命
voluntary	/ˈvɔləntəri/	adj. 自愿的
voyage	/ˈvɔiidʒ/	n. 航海，航行

W

whereas	/hwɛəˈæz/	conj. 而，却
worship	/ˈwəːʃip/	v. 崇拜，敬仰

Y

yield	/jiːld/	vt. 1.带来利益，生产 2.屈服

Z

zip code	/zipˌkəud/	n. 邮政编码

APPENDIX 4
International Airlines

各国及地区航空公司名称与代号

AA-American Airlines 美国航空

AC-Air Canada 加拿大航空

AF-Air France 法国航空

AI-Air India 印度航空

AZ-Alitalia 意大利航空

BA-British Airways 英国航空

CA-CACC-General Administration of Civil Aviation of China 中国民航

CI-China Airlines 中华航空

CO-Continental Airlines 大陆航空（美国）

CP-Canadian Pacific Airlines 加拿大太平洋航空

CX-Cathay Pacific Airways 国泰航空

DA-Hong Kong Dragon Airlines 港龙航空

DL-Delta Airlines 达美航空（美国）

EA-Eastern Airlines 东方航空

FR-Finnair 芬兰航空

GA-Gulf Air 海湾航空

JL-JAL-Japan Air Lines 日本航空

KE-Korean Air Lines 大韩航空

KL-KLM Royal Dutch Airlines 荷兰航空

LH-Lufthansa German Airlines 德国航空

MH-Malaysian Airline System 马来西亚航空

NH-All Nippon Airways 全日本航空

NW-Northwest Orient Airlines 西北航空

PR-Philippine Airlines 菲律宾航空

QF-Qantas Airways 澳洲航空

RG-VARIG Brazilian Airlines 巴西航空

SA-South African Airways 南非航空

SK-SAS-Scandinavian Airlines 北欧航空

SQ-Singapore Airlines 新加坡航空

SR-Swissair 瑞士航空
SV-Saudi Arabian Airlines 阿拉伯航空
TW-TWA-Trans World Airlines 环球航空(美国)
UA-United Airlines 联合航空(美国)

APPENDIX 5
Hotel Organizations Chart

饭店组织机构

1. General Manager's office 总经理室
   General Manager 总经理 Vice General Manager 副总经理
   General Manager's assistant 总经理助理
   Director of Executive Office 总经理办公室主任
   Executive Secretary 办公室秘书
2. Front Office 前厅部
   Front Office Manager 经理
   Front Office Assistant Manager or Lobby Assistant 大堂副理
   Reservationist 订房员 Receptionist 接待员
   Tour Coordinator 团体协调员 Doorman 门厅接应员
   Bell Captain 行李主管 Bellman 行李员
   Front Office Cashier 结帐员 Cashier 外币兑换员
   Operator 话务员 Information Clerk 问询员
   Mail Check 前厅收发员
3. Housekeeping Development 房务部
   Housekeeper 经理 Senior Supervisor 客房管理员
   Floor Supervisor 房务部领班 Floor Attendant 楼层服务员
   Room Attendant 客房服务员 Houseman 杂务工
   Valet 洗烫工 Linen Maid 物品保管员
4. Food and Beverage Department 餐饮部
   F. &. B Manager 餐饮部经理 Restaurant Supervisor 餐厅管理员
   Restaurant Captain 餐厅领班 Waitor/Waitress 餐厅服务员
   Restaurant Reservationist 餐厅预定员 Hostess 餐厅应接员
   Executive Chef 厨师长 Head Chef 厨房主管
   Cook 炉灶厨师 Butcher 切配厨师
   Chef 西餐厨师 Bartender 酒吧调酒师
   Barmen 酒吧服务员 Baker 面包房操作工
   Pastry Cook 点心工 Stoward 餐具管事
   Dishwasher 洗碟工 Busboy 助理服务员

5. Sales Department 销售部
    Sales Manager 经理 Sales Promotion Officer 推销员
6. Public Relations Department 公共关系部
    Public Relations Manager 经理 Public Relations Officer 公关员
7. Recreation Department 康乐部
    Recreation Department Manager 经理 Stage Attendan 舞厅服务员 t
    Gymnasium Attendant 健康房服务员 Bowling Attendant 保龄球房服务员
    Billiard Attendant 桌球房服务员 Sauna Attendant 桑拿浴室服务员
    Swimming Pool Attendant 游泳池服务员
    Beautician 美容员 Barber/Hair Dresser 理发师
    Masseur/Masseuse 按摩师
8. Store Department 商场部
    Sales Manager 经理 Supervisor 管理员
    Sales Clerk, Shop Assistant 营业员
9. Purchasing Department 采购部
    Purchasing Manager 经理
    Food Storeroom Supervisor 食品采购主管
    Food Buyer 食品采购员 Food Receiver 食品验收员
    Dry Food Storeman 食品干货保管员
    Engineering Storekeeper, General Goods Storeman 保管员(工程、总务)
    Engineering Buyer, General Goods Buyer 采购员
10. Financial Department 财务部
    Financial Controller 经理 Chief Accountant 主管
    Accounting Clerk 总帐报表员 Payroll Control 工资核算员
    Cashier 出纳员 Payable/Receivable Clerk 往来结算员
    Property Control 财产核算员 Cost Control 成本核算员
11. Security Department 保卫部
    Chief Security Officer 经理 Security Officer 安全保卫员
    Director of Fire Centre 消防中心主任 Fireman 消防员
    Guard 门卫 Patroller 巡逻员
12. Personnel Department 人事部
    Personnel Department Manager 经理 Payroll Master 劳动工资员
    Personnel Assistant 人事调配员
13. Engineering Department 工程维修部
    Chief Engineer 经理 Mechanician 机修工

Air-conditioning Man 空调工 Lift Man 电梯工
Boilerman 锅炉工 Carpetman 地毯壁纸工
Key Keeper 钥匙工

APPENDIX 6
Chinese Scenic Spots

中国风景名胜

1. 北京 Beijing
    长城—The Great Wall
    故宫—The Palace Museum（紫禁城—Forbidden City）
    颐和园—The Summer Palace
    圆明园—Ruins of the Old Summer Palace
    天坛—The Temple of Heaven
    鼓楼—The Drum Tower
    十三陵—Ming Tombs
    天安门—Tiananmen Square
    周口店北京人遗址—Peking Man Site at Zhoukoudian
2. 上海 Shanghai
    外滩—The Bund
    玉佛寺—Jade Buddha Temple
    豫园—Yuyuan Gardens
    上海大戏院—Shanghai Grand Theater
    城隍庙—City God Temple
3. 沈阳 Shenyang
    沈阳故宫—Shenyang Old Palace
    北陵公园—Beiling Park
4. 哈尔滨 Harbin
    索非亚大教堂—Sophia Cathedral
    中央大街—Central Avenue
    冰雪节—Ice and Snow Festival
    太阳岛—The Sun Island
5. 牡丹江 Mudanjiang
    镜泊湖—Jingpo Lake
    吊水楼瀑布—Diaoshuilou Waterfall
    地下森林—Underground Forest
6. 新疆 Xinjiang

天池—Lake Tianchi
7. 敦煌 Dunhuang
   莫高窟—Mogao Grottoes
   鸣沙山—Echoing-Sand Mountain
8. 拉萨 Lhasa
   布达拉宫—Potala Palace
9. 西安 Xi'an
   秦始皇兵马俑—The Emperor Qin's Terra-cotta Museum
   华清池—Huaqing Pool
   大雁塔—Big Wild Goose Pagoda
   小雁塔—Small Wild Goose Pagoda
10. 四川 Sichuan
    长江三峡—Three Gorges on the Changjiang River
    望江楼—Overlooking the river Tower
    峨眉山—Mount Emei
    杜甫草堂—Thatched Cottage of Du Fu
    九寨沟—Jiuzhaigou Valley
11. 桂林 Guilin
    骆驼山象鼻山—Camel Mountain and Elephant Trunk Hill
    漓江—Lijiang River
    七星岩—Sever-Star Cave
12. 江西 Jiangxi
    庐山—Mount Lushan
13. 福建 Fujian
    厦门鼓浪屿—Gulangyu Island of Xiamen
    日光岩—Rock of Sunshine
14. 安徽 Anhui
    黄山—Mount Huangshan
15. 湖北 Hubei
    黄鹤楼—Yellow Crane Tower
16. 山东 Shandong
    泰山—Mount Taishan
    趵突泉—Baotu Spring
    孔庙—The Confucius Temple
17. 无锡 Wuxi

太湖—Lake Taihu
18. 杭州 Hangzhou
    西湖—West Lake
    灵隐寺—Lingyin Buddhist Monastery
    岳王庙—Yue Fei's Temple and Tomb
19. 苏州 Suzhou
    拙政园—Humble Administrator's Garden
    狮子林—Lion Grove
    网狮园—Fisherman's Garden
    沧浪亭—Pavilion of the Surging Waves
    周庄古镇—Zhouzhuang Ancient Town
20. 南京 Nanjing
    中山陵—Dr. Sun Yat-sen's Mausoleum
    南京长江大桥—Nanjing Changjiang River Bridge
    玄武湖—Xuanwu Lake
    雨花台—Rain Flower Pebbles
    莫愁湖—Mochou Lake
21. 河南 Henan
    龙门石窟—The Longmen Grottoes
    少林寺—Shaolin Temple
    白马寺—White Horse Temple
22. 贵州 Guizhou
    黄果树瀑布—The Huanguoshu Falls
23. 云南 Yunnan
    昆明世博园—Kunming World Horti-Expo Garden
    石林—Stone Forest
    滇池—Dianchi Lake
    丽江古城—Lijiang Ancient Town
24. 湖南 Hunan
    岳阳楼—Yueyang Tower
25. 河北 Hebei
    承德避暑山庄—Chengde Mountain Resort
26. 海南 Hainan
    天涯海角—The Edge of Sky and the Rim of Sea